BIOETHICS AND THE HUMAN GOODS

V

D0775396

Bioethics and the human
goods : an introduction
to natural law bioethics
33305234667560
5an   02/17/16

BIOETHICS AND THE HUMAN GOODS

An Introduction to Natural Law Bioethics

Alfonso Gómez-Lobo

with John Keown

GEORGETOWN UNIVERSITY PRESS / WASHINGTON, DC

© 2015 Georgetown University Press. All rights reserved. No part of this book may be reproduced or utilized in any form or by any means, electronic or mechanical, including photocopying and recording, or by any information storage and retrieval system, without permission in writing from the publisher.

Library of Congress Cataloging-in-Publication Data

Gómez-Lobo, Alfonso, 1940– author.
Bioethics and the human goods : an introduction to natural law bioethics / Alfonso Gómez-Lobo ; with John Keown.
pages cm
Includes bibliographical references and index.
ISBN 978-1-62616-163-4 (pb : alk. paper) — ISBN 978-1-62616-271-6 (hc : alk. paper) — ISBN 978-1-62616-164-1 (eb)
1. Bioethics. 2. Natural law. I. Keown, John, author. II. Title.
QH332.G65 2015
174.2—dc23
2015001489

∞ This book is printed on acid-free paper meeting the requirements of the American National Standard for Permanence in Paper for Printed Library Materials.

16 15   9 8 7 6 5 4 3 2 First printing
Printed in the United States of America

Cover design by N. Putens.

To my wife, Jimena, and our children,
Veronica, Andrés, Jimena, and Rosario

CONTENTS

PREFACE

This book was largely written by the late Alfonso Gómez-Lobo, Ryan Professor of Metaphysics and Moral Philosophy at Georgetown University.[1] He was an eminent scholar, beloved teacher, and cherished colleague. His loss was, and remains, keenly felt, both at Georgetown and at the Pontifical Catholic University of Chile, where he was a visiting professor. An authority on classical Greek philosophy (he was fluent in ancient and modern Greek as well as six other languages), he was also an expert on bioethics. His expertise was recognized by the president of the United States, George W. Bush, who appointed him to the President's Council on Bioethics.[2]

Gómez-Lobo died at the close of 2011. He left an unpublished manuscript on bioethics, which he had submitted to Georgetown University Press. The press had commissioned three referees' reports. Although he had replied to these reports, his final illness prevented his completion of the project. My goal in completing his project has been, broadly, to finish it in the way he indicated in his response to the referees' reports that he intended to finish it and, where he left no indication, to finish it in the way I think he would have finished it or at least would not have objected to it being finished. I have also made a number of relatively minor changes of my own, such as the addition of definitions, examples that illustrate points made in the text, and a bibliography. I have also added an appendix containing personal statements to the President's Council by Gómez-Lobo on the status of the human embryo and on the determination of death, statements that flesh out his views on those matters. I have amended the work to take account of a number of developments since the original manuscript was written and have made some stylistic changes and changes of emphasis and nuance. However, I have neither added nor subtracted anything fundamental. The finished product remains largely the work of Gómez-Lobo. About a third of the book is material I have written.

There are precious few texts introducing students with an interest in bioethics—whether students of philosophy, medicine, or law—to the "natural law" approach to ethical reflection. Given the deep, historical influence of that tradition on Western political, legal, and moral philosophy and, more particularly for our purposes, on professional medical ethics and the law governing medical practice (not least the criminal law), this dearth is regrettable. It is doubly regrettable given the growing importance of bioethics in educational curricula, whether in university, college, or high school, and to modern society.

Recent years have witnessed the welcome publication of several books and papers reflecting a renaissance of interest in ethics or morality (in this book the two terms are used interchangeably) from a natural law perspective. Much of this literature is, however, aimed at academics.[3] There are few works of an introductory nature aimed at the general reader. Gómez-Lobo's excellent introductory book *Morality and the Human Goods* is an exception (2002). Moreover, although the literature on bioethics is vast, there is only a handful of books on bioethics that adopt a natural law perspective, and although they are impressive works, they tend to deal with specific issues such as research on human embryos or abortion.[4] There is, then, something of a void facing the college student or the intelligent general reader who wants a clear, basic introduction to bioethical theory and its application to a number of key life and death issues from a natural law perspective.

To make matters worse, natural law, to the very limited extent that the enormous literature on bioethics mentions it at all, is more often than not misunderstood and caricatured. Natural law is often summarily dismissed as "religious," or as based on the belief that "what is right is a matter of following natural inclinations," or as holding that "any interference with natural processes is wrong." Though it is fair to say that some natural lawyers over the centuries have expressed themselves using terminology that invites such criticisms, the criticisms are nevertheless misguided.

Let us take just the first misunderstanding, that natural law is "religious." It is true that natural law has historically been the philosophical tradition adopted by the Christian Church and that many of its leading exponents have been in the past, and are today, Catholic Christians. However, natural law has its origins in pre-Christian Greek philosophy, and it remains to this day a philosophy, not a theology. It can therefore—like human rights and social justice (which are also strongly defended by Catholic thinkers)—be adopted by anyone, whether or not they subscribe to Catholicism, Christianity, or indeed any faith tradition. Would the US Congress have been justified in dismissing Martin

Luther King Jr.'s campaign for civil rights for African Americans, which invoked natural law, because he was a minister of the Christian religion?[5]

Many religious believers, particularly but by no means only those in the Judeo-Christian tradition, will have parallel theological reasons for agreeing with or sympathizing with natural law ethics, especially its emphasis on respecting the equal dignity of *all* human beings, not least the vulnerable, such as the very young, and the marginalized, like the very old. But the ethical theory and arguments outlined in this book are based on reason, not faith.

When it comes to introductory, informed books on natural law, particularly in relation to bioethics, the void is, then, as great as the need. It is to be hoped that this short book will help to fill the void and meet the need by introducing the reader to the foundations of natural law theory in relation to bioethics, and to the application of that theory to some of the key issues at the beginning and end of life. Its sister book, *Morality and the Human Goods*, which could profitably be read before this one, offered a short introduction to natural law ethics. This book offers a short introduction to natural law bioethics. It does not attempt a deep, scholarly exposition of natural law theory, or to address all the differences and nuances of opinion between natural law thinkers on bioethical issues, still less to explore the veritable host of complex bioethical issues facing the contemporary world, especially in developed societies. Nor does it contain copious citations to the vast literature in bioethics; it is lightly annotated. It contents itself with citations to some important contemporary texts on natural law bioethics, as well as some leading sources which take a different view.

The book introduces the reader to a way of thinking that in the view of Gómez-Lobo and several other expert bioethicists, such as Dr. Edmund Pellegrino (the "Father of Bioethics"), offers the soundest approach to bioethics. It is an approach grounded in a recognition of the fundamental equality-in-dignity of each and every human being. It holds, in concord with the Preamble of the Universal Declaration of Human Rights, that "recognition of the inherent dignity and of the equal and inalienable rights of all members of the human family is the foundation of freedom, justice and peace in the world."[6] It is an approach that—in contrast to the "utilitarian" or "ends justify the means" approach to ethics that is in one form or another now so influential in many universities and colleges—refuses to regard any human being as expendable or disposable, as a mere means to the "autonomous" wishes of others or to their "greater happiness," or to the "greater good" of society. Similarly, in contrast to the "principlist" approach to bioethics, which is scarcely less influential than utilitarianism, it refuses to allow any human being to be afforded less protection than others or to be used as a mere means to the ends of others on the basis of a controversial interpretation and application of the four ethical principles of nonmaleficence, beneficence, justice, and respect for autonomy. This book will sketch a natural law interpretation and application of those principles. Moreover, although those principles, properly understood, are a vital part of a sound bioethics, they are by no means exhaustive.

Natural law is an approach that, in line with the Hippocratic tradition of medical ethics, which has shaped medical ethics for centuries and which—although increasingly challenged by utilitarian and principlist thinking—to a significant extent still does, holds that some ways of dealing with patients (such as intentionally killing them, exploiting them, or lying to them) are always and everywhere wrong, regardless of the good consequences that such conduct may bring about.[7]

Whether, before or after reading this book, you are persuaded by natural law ethics or not, you should at least end up better informed about an approach to ethical reflection that has profoundly shaped Western medicine, law, and society.[8] That goal was, I am sure, what inspired Alfonso Gómez-Lobo to embark on this work.

John Keown

Notes

1. A short biography of Gómez-Lobo is found on Wikipedia, http://en.wikipedia.org/wiki/Alfonso_G%C3%B3mez-Lobo. His video-recorded testimony to the Maryland House of Delegates against the proposed funding of research on human embryos is available on YouTube, "Prof Alfonso Gomez-Lobo vs embryonic stem cell research," http://www.youtube.com/watch?v=450eZU5qU4g.

2. This prestigious council was chaired in turn by two eminent physician-philosophers: first, Dr. Leon Kass of the University of Chicago and, later, Dr. Edmund Pellegrino, founding director of the Center for Clinical Bioethics at Georgetown University (now the Pellegrino Center). For some of the Council's publications, see the President's Council on Bioethics entries in the references. A few of Dr. Pellegrino's many publications are also listed in the references.

3. See for example Finnis (2011b). John Finnis, a preeminent authority on law and philosophy, has been largely responsible, with his collaborators Germain Grisez and Joseph Boyle, for the contemporary renaissance of natural law philosophy. See generally Keown and George (2013). For a lucid, concise overview of Finnis's natural law approach to bioethics, see Fisher (2013).

4. See, for example, Beckwith (2007); Lee (2010); George and Tollefsen (2011); Kaczor (2015). For more general books, see Fitzpatrick (1988); Oderberg (2000a, 2000b); Watt (2000); Tollefsen (2008); Spitzer (2011); Napier (2011); Kaczor (2013).

5. See, for example, King (1963), where he wrote: "To put it in the terms of Saint Thomas Aquinas, an unjust law is a human law that is not rooted in eternal and natural law. Any law that uplifts human personality is just. Any law that degrades human personality is unjust. All segregation statutes are unjust because segregation distorts the soul and damages the personality" (7).

6. United Nations, "The Universal Declaration of Human Rights," http://www.un.org/en/documents/udhr/ (1948).

7. The Oath of Hippocrates (460–375 BC) prohibited abortion and physician-assisted suicide. See National Institutes of Health, "Greek Medicine: The Hippocratic Oath," http://www.nlm.nih.gov/hmd/greek/greek_oath.html. Until relatively recently in the history of medicine, abortion was condemned by the medical profession as a whole. Physician-assisted suicide still is.

8. It should not be assumed that natural law ethics is only of relevance to the West, not least because if the claims of natural law ethics are true, they are valid universally. On the compatibility of natural law with Buddhist ethics, see Keown (2001). For a Jewish perspective, see Novak (2007).

ACKNOWLEDGMENTS

I should like to thank Mrs. Jimena Gómez-Lobo for her kind permission to complete her late husband's work.

Thanks are also due to Richard Brown, the director of Georgetown University Press, for welcoming my proposal to complete it and to the board of the Press for approving it, and I am grateful (as was Professor Gómez-Lobo) to the three anonymous referees of his original manuscript for their comments and suggestions.

I am also indebted to Professors John Finnis, Christopher Kaczor, Damien Keown, Melissa Moschella, and Christopher Tollefsen, who read and commented upon earlier or later versions of the revised manuscript. It should not be assumed that they (or, indeed, I) necessarily agree with everything in it. Lauren Saunee and Alyson Cox helped check the references. Professor Robert George kindly approved the inclusion in the appendix of his joint statement with Professor Gómez-Lobo.

Finally, most of my work on the book was carried out at the Center for Ethics and Culture at the University of Notre Dame du Lac, where I held the Remick Senior Fellowship while on sabbatical leave from Georgetown University. I am grateful to Georgetown for granting me leave and to the director of the Center for Ethics and Culture, Professor Carter Snead, and his staff for generously providing me with such a welcoming and congenial sabbatical environment.

John Keown

INTRODUCTION

The *Oxford English Dictionary* defines bioethics as "the discipline deal-ing with ethical issues relating to the practice of medicine and biology or arising from advances in these subjects."[1] In one sense, it is a fairly new field that has become prominent due to the remarkable techno-logical progress of recent decades. New biomedical technologies affect life in ways that were hitherto unimaginable. There is, for example, in vitro fertilization (IVF), in which a woman's egg is fertilized by a man's sperm in vitro ("in glass") in the laboratory. Since the birth of the first "test-tube" baby in the United Kingdom in 1978, this technology has led to the births of millions of babies worldwide (Frith 2014). It has also generated a plethora of bioethical questions.

Millions more embryos created in vitro have never been implanted in a woman than have been born.[2] Moreover, IVF technology has been developed through research involving the destruction of countless hu-man embryos. Is such research ethical? The practice of IVF to provide babies for infertile couples typically involves the discarding of human embryos either because they are "spare" (i.e., surplus to requirements) or because they are judged "defective" and therefore unsuitable for im-plantation in a woman. It also involves the storage of many human em-bryos in freezers until such time as they may, or may not, be wanted for some use. Is it ethical to destroy or discard human embryos or to keep them in "suspended animation"? And, even if no embryo were destroyed, discarded, or frozen, would it be ethical to create human life in the laboratory, or would it be objectionable because it would be treat-ing human procreation like product manufacture? Again, is it ethical for a couple to pay another woman to gestate their embryo (surrogate motherhood); for rich couples to pay poor women for their eggs; or to create a child for A, with an egg donated by B and a sperm donated by C, to be gestated by D? Should unborn babies be aborted if disabled, or if the continuation of the pregnancy would involve a risk to the mother's life or health, or if they are simply unwanted? Should babies born very prematurely be placed in incubators or left to die? Should babies born with serious disabilities be given lethal injections? The list of bioethi-cal questions goes on. Whereas IVF produces embryos by combining a

woman's egg and a man's sperm in the laboratory, another technological development allows embryos to be created in the laboratory without
even the male sperm—cloning. As the birth of Dolly the sheep dramati-
cally demonstrated in 1996, scientists can now clone mammals.[3] The
technology involves removing the nucleus from a female mammal's egg
and replacing it with the nucleus from another cell, such as a skin cell
(whether taken from another animal or from the female herself), to
produce a virtually identical copy of the animal that donated the cell
nucleus. The science of mammalian cloning is still in its infancy, but
it will surely not be very long before scientists are able to improve and
perhaps perfect that technology and then turn their attention to the
cloning of human beings. Would it be ethical to clone human beings? If
so, in what circumstances? To create a child for a couple where the man
cannot produce sperm? To replace a beloved child killed in an accident?
To replicate a revered political leader?

At the other end of life, too, technology has provoked a range of bioethical questions. With the use of artificial ventilators, it is now possible
to keep people alive even though they cannot breathe on their own. If
the patient is permanently unconscious, is it ethical to switch the machine off? Does it make any difference if, before becoming unconscious,
the patient declared that they would not want to be kept alive in such
a condition? Or if the patient is pregnant and maintaining ventilation
for several months would allow the baby to be born and survive? Is a
patient who is permanently comatose "alive" or "dead"? If a patient on
a ventilator is conscious but asks for it to be removed because they do
not want to live connected to a ventilator, is it ethical to remove it even
though the patient will immediately die? If it is right to remove a ventilator from a permanently unconscious patient who cannot breathe on
their own, is it right to remove tube feeding from such a patient who
can breathe on their own? Modern medical technology has raised many
difficult ethical questions at both the beginning and end of life.

On the other hand, human conduct has always had the ability to
affect life, either positively or negatively; thus, bioethics—albeit by another name—has existed for quite some time. Some of the contemporary questions of bioethics are essentially old questions in a new form.
For example, people have wondered in the past whether a disabled
newborn baby should be left to die, or whether the life of a seriously ill
person should be prolonged at all costs. The technological means to be

used, or not used, in such cases may have changed, but the underlying moral issues are essentially the same. And are some questions really a result of new technology? What is technologically new about feeding an unconscious patient through a tube?

There is a narrower field than bioethics—namely, medical ethics. From the origins of medicine in ancient Greece, physicians have explored ethical questions relating to its practice. The product of their reflections has been the formulation of an evolving body of ethical norms or standards of proper conduct. Those contained in the Hippocratic Oath have been doubtless the best known and the most influential on subsequent generations. Today many writers continue to address general bioethical questions in connection with specific questions of medical ethics, thus generating the field aptly called "biomedical ethics." It is laudable, of course, to develop an abstract philosophical discipline and to have at the same time the practical aim of being of service to the practitioners of the medical art. The latter is also one of the aims of this book.

It is wise, however, to draw a clear conceptual distinction between bioethics and medical ethics. Whereas medical ethics concerns ethical questions arising in the context of the doctor–patient relationship, bioethics ranges more widely. For example, those researching on or cloning human embryos may well be scientists rather than physicians, and their contact with an individual patient may be nonexistent. Since the primary duty of a doctor is to heal and comfort an individual patient, it is hardly surprising that the virtues (i.e., good character traits or dispositions) traditionally associated with the practice of medicine have a limited role to play in a laboratory engaged in pure biomedical research.[4] Medical ethics rightly focuses on the moral requirements within a particular profession, whereas bioethics unavoidably deals also with issues of a more general nature.

In this book the primary goal is to develop a broad conception of bioethics that also seeks to provide a foundation for medical ethics and for other practices, professions, and activities that directly affect human life (at least in the biomedical context). As the book progresses, it should become clear that the foundations of bioethics, in turn, are to be found in two more basic philosophical disciplines: ethics and ontology. Ethics is a normative discipline that attempts to determine at the most general level which human actions are morally right and which are wrong. Ontology, on the other hand, is a descriptive discipline that seeks to identify what something is, its nature. Ethics considers: "Is it right or wrong to treat X in a particular way?" Ontology considers: "What *is* X? A person? A thing? Something else?" Many philosophers would hold that before we can decide how we ought to treat X, we should first consider who, or what, X is: what *kind* of being. The moral question whether a hunter is right to shoot at something moving in the bushes surely depends on whether that something moving is a warthog or his wife. Ontology is particularly important in bioethics because many central disagreements are ultimately disagreements about what certain organisms are. For example, is the in vitro human embryo a person, a thing, or something else? Is a patient in a persistent vegetative state (PVS) a person, a vegetable, or something else?

But why "bioethics and the human goods"? One reason this book accords human goods such a prominent position is to indicate its contrast with one of the most influential books in bioethics today, namely, *Principles of Biomedical Ethics* by Tom Beauchamp and James Childress (2013). This is a leading work that is considered canonical in many parts of the world. It advocates and expounds a "principlist" approach to bioethics. Beauchamp and Childress propose and defend the idea that biomedical ethics should be governed by four principles of equal importance: respect for autonomy, nonmaleficence, beneficence, and justice. However, this approach suffers from a serious underlying problem. Since nonmaleficence enjoins us not to harm people and beneficence exhorts us to benefit others, any application of these principles logically requires a prior conception of "the good" that can provide criteria to determine what is "harmful" and what is "beneficial." If a person does not have a firm grasp of the human good(s), how can she argue with any assurance that her contemplated action will harm or benefit someone on the receiving end of her action? How can one judge correct and incorrect claims of beneficence or no-maleficence? In line with many writers in the modern liberal tradition, Beauchamp and Childress do not provide a theory of the human goods, and this leaves a significant gap in the foundation of their approach.[5]

Many philosophers both ancient and modern are convinced that the prior identification of the good or the goods should be the cornerstone of ethics because morality, as commonly understood, is a social institution whose goal is the protection and promotion of things that are good for humans. Aristotle's strict condemnation of adultery and murder, for example, becomes intelligible only if we assume that he considered marriage and life to be basic goods that ought always to be protected.[6]

There is indeed a long tradition in philosophy going back to the ancient Greeks that takes a set of human goods as axiomatic and justifies the general moral norms (i.e., standards of proper moral conduct) by reference to those goods. A contemporary version of that approach to general ethics is provided in *Morality and the Human Goods*, which was written for students, professionals, and other readers who are not formally trained in philosophy (Gómez-Lobo 2002). *Bioethics and the Human Goods* takes a similar approach, with the aim that it be fruitfully read both by nonspecialized readers and by health care professionals who feel confused by the contradictory views that emerge from the vast body of contemporary bioethical writings. This book is a reliable and self-contained introduction to bioethics that does not abandon the main positions of traditional Western ethics under the pressure exerted by the demands of modern biotechnology or yield to the challenges presented by other philosophical approaches like principlism and utilitarianism. The natural law positions should not be invoked dogmatically, of course, and must be defended, by reason, in their own right.

By its very nature this is not a "neutral" book. Its aim is not to present all the different positions on the issues without preferring any. Few (if any) books on bioethics manage to do this. Indeed, many textbooks and anthologies that profess neutrality in fact contain an undisclosed (and sometimes perhaps unconscious) bias in their selection of the material or in the way in which the different extracts are introduced.[7] The approach here is to explain and defend the natural law ethical position on certain issues of life and death. The vast majority of books on bioethics present alternative approaches, typically either principlist or utilitarian.[8]

The natural law perspective on bioethics is, then, a minority view in the field of bioethics. However, the key question must be whether it is true, not whether the majority of bioethicists subscribe to it. Majorities are often wrong. And with the current emphasis in universities on the importance of diversity, it is to be hoped that greater attention will be given to this minority and widely neglected approach, not least given its historical importance in forming Western medical ethics and law. Indeed, it is difficult to see how any student could have a proper understanding of the foundations of Western ethics and law without at least *some* appreciation of natural law thought.

Although this book is an introduction to bioethics and its medical applications from a natural law perspective, no effort is made to address and resolve many of the more complex, difficult dilemmas that can arise in medical practice. In such cases the correct (or, as is often the case, the least defective) solution is often a function of a host of circumstances that have to be taken into account by the person or persons responsible for the particular decision. The multiple variables that can arise in individual cases resist adequate treatment in the setting of an introductory book like this. It is also often the case that because of the complexity of the circumstances, none of the two (or more) available choices may in fact be seriously wrong, or wrong at all. Nor does this book seek to identify, let alone explore, all the differences—sometimes significant differences—that exist between bioethicists *within* the natural law tradition.

What is important is that doctors and others should possess a sure, basic grasp of the norms and principles of natural law bioethics in light of which cases, including difficult cases, should be approached and decided. The modest goal of this book is to offer a clarification of those norms and principles. The analytical framework adopted in this book will be the same four principles at the heart of the influential principlist approach to bioethics—nonmaleficence, beneficence, justice, and respect for autonomy. These principles will be interpreted and applied from a natural law perspective. This is not to suggest that these four principles exhaust natural law bioethics; far from it (see Finnis and Fisher 1994). But they are of central importance, and it should be helpful to the reader, given the widespread popularity of the principlist approach, to see how those principles are broadly understood and applied in natural law bioethics.

No human being manages to live in perfect compliance with the demands of morality. Sometimes people break the moral norms and are willing to admit it. But sometimes people search for rationalizations that consist in carving out exceptions to, rather than in a wholesale rejection of, well-established norms and principles. Most people would agree that torture should not be used in police interrogation, but many people would be willing to admit an exception in the case of a terrorist suspect. Most people would agree that adultery is morally wrong, but some people think that a discreet and brief affair (especially if they themselves are engaging in one) is acceptable. The same line of thought is often evident in relation to contemporary bioethical issues: certain traditional principles are respected but with a tendency to admit exceptions. Most people would agree that physicians should not kill their patients, but many people think that in certain particular circumstances physicians should carry out "euthanasia" and administer a lethal injection to end suffering, at least if the patient has requested it. Most people agree that infanticide is wrong, but some people argue that in certain cases killing an infant is permissible, such as when a child has been born missing much of its brain and has only days to live, and when its vital organs, if taken now, could save the lives of other infants.

Such exceptions are often partly justified by emphasizing a factor not mentioned by the general norm such as, in the case of euthanasia, the presence of excruciating pain and, in the case of the killing of seriously disabled newborns, the need for organs for transplantation. It is also partly achieved by weakening the principle or norm itself. If the rationale for a moral rule is obscured or not fully understood, then it is only natural to think that absolute fidelity to a certain moral norm is merely "rule worship," that is, a determination to uphold the rule simply for the rule's sake. The admission of exceptions, even multiple exceptions, will then seem apposite.

Careful reflection both on the external factors invoked to justify exceptions and on the force of the norm can, however, show them to be linked to some good or evil. It is on those links that this book hopes to shed some light and thereby help to answer the difficult question of whether the common tendency to admit exceptions is ethical progress or, rather, ethical regress.

Let us now turn to a particular kind of action that has over the last thirty years, particularly the last fifteen years or so, been the subject of intense bioethical dispute—research on human embryos in vitro. We shall consider whether such research is morally justified or unjustified and, if justified, whether justified by a rule or as an exception to a rule.

Notes

1. Although the issues considered in this book largely arise in the context of the doctor–patient relationship, bioethics is not so limited. It extends, for ex-

ample, to the question of justice in the allocation of health care resources. For an examination of this from a natural law perspective, see Fisher and Gormally (2001). Some bioethicists understand bioethics as extending to our treatment of the environment (at least insofar as it impacts life and health). See, for example, Madison Powers, "FEW Resources.org," http://www.fewresources.org/about -this-site.html. *Oxford English Dictionary*, 3rd ed., November 2010.

2. For official statistics from the United Kingdom, see Hough (2012).

3. Roslin Institute, "A Life of Dolly," http://www.roslin.ed.ac.uk/public-in terest/dolly-the-sheep/a-life-of-dolly/. See also President's Council on Bioethics (2002), chap. 4.

4. On virtue ethics in medicine, see Pellegrino and Thomasma (1993).

5. For a useful introduction to the principlist approach, see Gillon (1986). For an extensive treatment by advocates and critics, see Gillon (1994).

6. Aristotle *Nicomachean Ethics* II.6. 1107a 11–15. doi:10.4159/DLCL.aristo tle-nicomachean_ethics.1926.

7. One good example is a leading text in the United Kingdom on medical law and ethics: Kennedy and Grubb (1994). For a critical review of the book's bioethical selectivity, see Keown (1995). It is not surprising, given the influence of such books, that natural law ethics is misunderstood by many, including eminent lawyers and judges. See generally Keown (2012).

8. In addition to Beauchamp and Childress (2013), see, for example, Glover (1991); McMahan (2002); and Singer (2011).

Part I
FOUNDATIONS

Chapter 1
BIOETHICAL THINKING

Stella, a research scientist, arrives at work early in the morning and changes into her white lab coat. She opens the freezer and removes a container. Inside the container are six human embryos that have been shipped from a fertility clinic the day before. They are so-called spare embryos, left over from fertility treatment at the clinic. Fred and Sandra, who had been trying without success for two years to have a baby through sexual intercourse, had gone to the clinic to seek help, and the clinic had recommended in vitro fertilization (IVF). Ten embryos were created by mixing Sandra's eggs with Fred's sperm. All ten were examined under a microscope. Two were judged defective and left to one side to die. The other eight were judged to be of adequate quality, and two of those embryos were implanted into Sandra's womb. Fred and Sandra asked for the remaining six, the "spares," to be donated for scientific research, as they were "surplus to requirements."

Stella is engaged in a research project into embryonic stem cell research. These cells are special: they have the power to differentiate into other types of cells, such as skin cells and liver cells. Stem cells can be found in early embryos and in adult human beings.[1] But Stella's research involves stem cells taken from embryos, not adults. Stella hopes that by studying embryonic stem cells, she, together with other scientists involved in such research, will eventually be able to help doctors use them to treat patients who suffer from diseases like diabetes or cancer or Alzheimer's. But the research inevitably involves the destruction of the human embryos. Should Stella, as part of her research project, proceed to disaggregate the embryos in order to extract their stem cells even though this will destroy the embryos? Some will reply that she should proceed because what she is about to do is morally permissible. Others, however, will answer that it is seriously immoral. How can one decide with some degree of confidence which of these two answers is correct? We need first to analyze the action itself and then assess it from a moral point of view.

The analysis of the action can be said to be an exercise in—or application of—what philosophers call the "theory of action" or "action theory." This is a descriptive discipline that attempts to make an action intelligible by identifying the person who is acting (the agent), the point of the action, the intention of the agent, and the circumstances in which it is performed (Gómez-Lobo 2002, chap. 5). If we do not know who performs a certain action or what exactly it consists in, we may very well fail to understand it. Likewise, knowing what the agent intends and when and where the action is performed may also be crucial in reaching a correct understanding of what, precisely, is being done.

These inquiries (Who? What? Why? In what circumstances?) do not tell us that an action is right, acceptable, or permissible; that it is desirable; or that it is good that it be performed. In action theory we do not pass judgment, and we do not assign blame or praise. We dissect a whole and divide it into its constituent elements in order to understand it. It is simply an attempt to grasp what is or has been done. Action theory certainly involves more abstract ingredients because it presupposes some general understanding of what it is to be an agent (and not just someone advising an agent or following orders from an agent); of what constitutes in general the core of an action (as opposed to its peripheral elements); and, above all, of what it means for an agent to intend and not merely to foresee the consequences of his or her action.

In bioethics it may not be necessary to explore the abstract ingredients of action theory so long as we can successfully accomplish what is needed at the more particular level. In the example at hand we understand that the agent, Stella, is the researcher (and not one of the lab assistants or lab cleaners); that the action is the dismantling of human embryos; that the agent intends to extract embryonic stem cells with the further goal of making progress in biomedical research (and not for frivolous reasons), and that she is in the appropriate setting for doing the work (she is not engaged in rogue experiments in her garage without institutional approval). None of these observations settle the bioethical question. Indeed, we may ask: What is the bioethical question in the first place? Insofar as it is an ethical question it is twofold: it is a question about an *action*, and it is a question about an *agent*.

Ethical questions about the agent who performs an action are questions of responsibility, of blame or praise. A judgment about an agent's blameworthiness depends on various factors, including what the agent

knew, what she intended (in the ordinary sense of what her aim or purpose was), and what she chose to do. Everyone should act according
to his or her conscience. This is not to say that because a judgment is
made conscientiously it is therefore morally right. Slave owners may
have conscientiously thought they were right to own slaves. Nazis may
have conscientiously thought they were right to gas Jews. We can still
judge that, whether or not the agent was personally blameworthy, her
action was wrong. Moreover, an agent may be blameworthy in the way
she arrives at her conscientious judgment; for example, she may have
overlooked matters she should have taken into account. Many conscientious judgments are carelessly made.

How does one judge an action from a moral point of view? The
moral point of view is not the only alternative. We often judge actions
(our own and those of others) from a prudential point of view. The
prudential point of view is adopted when the primary consideration is
the benefit or the interests of the agent. When one parks one's car, it is
imprudent to leave valuables in view. When it is icy underfoot, it is imprudent to wear slippery soles. If Stella, the researcher in our example,
is working with funds from a grant awarded specifically to research on
embryonic stem cells, it might be imprudent for her to refuse to disaggregate the embryos. Her grant may be withdrawn and she may even
lose her job. Whether an action is or is not morally correct clearly does
not depend on prudential considerations.[2] If a person says, "This is correct because it is in my best interests," she would be giving a justification that few if any would accept. In deciding moral permissibility, the
primary criterion is clearly not simply benefit to the agent.

Some philosophers have held that moral permissibility is strictly a
function of the features of the particular case. Taken to the extreme,
this view entails the claim that one can "see" that this concrete action
was right and that the other one was wrong. Sometimes the technical
term "casuistry" is used to describe a method in ethics that starts in this
manner from "considered opinions" about particular kinds of action,
real or imagined, and then makes similar opinions about larger classes
of action. This is a "bottom-up" or inductive conception of morality. A
person directly observing Stella may instantly reach the conviction that
she is doing nothing wrong. She is just extracting stem cells. If other
researchers do the same thing, so the thinking goes, they also would not
be doing anything wrong. The end step in this inductive way of ethical

reasoning would be to make a general claim about actions of this sort: extracting stem cells from human embryos is ethical.

However, this approach to moral reasoning is flawed. The method relies heavily on an analogy with a method of scientific thinking that starts from direct observation. Multiple observations of particular instances of a phenomenon may lead to a reliable generalization, and this is possible because sensible properties are perceptible and for the most part measurable, either directly or by means of instruments. Moral properties, on the other hand, are neither perceptible nor measurable. If X claims that a particular action is "wrong," X cannot justify that claim by appeal to something X perceives, in the way that X could do if X claimed that something was "hot." The terms "hot" and "wrong" stand for very different sorts of property. X can justifiably claim that a given object is hot because that is how it affects X's touch or registers a temperature on a thermometer. But X cannot justifiably claim that an action is wrong because X *feels* it is wrong or can somehow *measure* its wrongness. There is no such thing as a moral thermometer. Slave owners felt it was right to own slaves. Nazis felt it was right to gas Jews. Did those feelings make their actions right?

Sometimes observation or consideration of a particular action may be followed by reflection, and the conviction that it was right or wrong may be reached after some time has elapsed. This is what we usually call "a considered opinion." Although it may seem that a considered opinion has been drawn exclusively from the particulars of the case, in fact a more general ingredient is necessarily involved, for by its very structure a considered opinion is a judgment. To judge, for example, that a particular defendant is guilty of a crime is to hold that on a specified occasion he broke the law, and the law is a set of general rules.

A swift moral judgment may be passed with little or no reflection on the fact that one is subsuming or bringing a case under a rule. In fact, it often happens that the pertinent rule, such as the wrongness of rape, has been internalized long ago through education or because of the prevalence of that rule in the culture, and this contributes to the mistaken impression that the morality of what was done can be "read off" the particulars of the action itself. The fact that judgment may be swift and involve little reflection does not mean there was no judgment at all and that there was merely moral "feeling" or "intuition."

A good reason to deny that we have such direct intuitions and insights comes from the fact that in our exchanges in real life we demand that allegedly intuitive claims be justified. If X says that it seems to him intuitively correct for Dr. M to treat patient P without consent, you can always ask "Why?" X will probably say, for example, that P has the Ebola virus and treatment is justified to prevent its spread to the community. If X provides some such justification for his intuition, he has gone beyond the particular case. X has made explicit the rule under which tacitly, and even perhaps unconsciously, he subsumed or brought the case. Not to do so would be to misunderstand how we use the terms "right" and "wrong" when we talk to each other. Both terms demand reasoned justification from a general perspective, not just personal feelings or intuitions. It may of course be that our judgments confirm our intuitions, but they may not. In any event, our moral judgments should rest on reason, not feeling.

If the appeal to rules is built into our moral language, then the next step in our ethical reflection about Stella's research must be to face the following question: Is there a rule or norm that prohibits or allows the dismantling of human embryos? The question is ambiguous. In one sense it asks whether there are *accepted* moral norms of what philosophers have sometimes called *positive* morality that bear on this issue. Moral norms do not exist in the same way in which horses exist and centaurs do not exist—that is, as objects in space and time. Norms exist only as rules for action that are thought about, whether with acceptance or rejection, by a particular human community. If we take a narrow view of community and ask whether the natives of a remote area in the Amazon basin have a norm about the proper treatment of human embryos, we embark on a futile inquiry because they have not achieved the technological level that makes the action under scrutiny feasible. Surely, if an action is not feasible for the members of a human group, they will have no reason to formulate a general rule to govern it. If we take a broader notion of community, such as to embrace, say, all countries that possess a level of scientific development that allows them to fertilize human eggs in vitro, we are likely to find conflicting norms of positive morality: some countries pass laws banning human embryo research, others pass laws funding it.

Are there, in contrast to norms of positive morality, norms of *critical* morality—that is, norms that are true regardless of whether any community or, indeed, anyone at all accepts them? Historically, many philosophers have taken the view that there is, indeed, a morality that transcends particular cultural communities, a "common morality" consisting of a set of general moral norms that are truths about fully reasonable action. These truths of morality exist, rather like truths of logic or scientific method or history exist, as awaiting discovery and acceptance as guides to right thinking, to right conscientious judgment and fully reasonable choices of action. These moral norms have been accepted, even if only in varying and distorted forms, by human communities supranationally through the ages, but their truth no more depends on their being accepted than do the truths of logic, science, or history. In earlier times this morality that we experience as common was called the "natural law" in contrast to "civil law."[3] Civil laws, like the law in Indiana prohibiting theft, or the law in the United Kingdom against driving over seventy miles per hour, are created in a particular jurisdiction at a particular time. The natural law, by contrast, concerns moral truths. (So, natural "law" is a potentially misleading term: it would be more helpful if it were called natural "ethics," but the label is now probably too established to change.) Both common morality and the natural law are conceived as normative and universally binding (even when not universally accepted) so that no practice within a group or country or culture can claim to be justified only because it is a practice of the group or the culture. For example, a country that claims that female genital mutilation is acceptable because it is part of its national tradition should surely be condemned from the perspective of the common or universal morality.[4]

But of what does the common or universal morality consist? A standard reply consists in giving a list of norms such as "Do not lie," "Do not steal," "Do not kill," "Do not neglect the young and dependent," "Do not commit adultery," and so on. The lists, both traditional and recent, will vary somewhat, but no list will include a norm dealing with stem cell extraction from human embryos. This is a new practice in which very few individuals will engage and, hence, cannot be expected to have been the subject matter of historic reflection within any community. One approach would be to formulate a new rule allowing embryo destruction and then to bring it under a general moral principle that bids us to do good: the principle of beneficence. Since embryo research aims at the healing of the sick and the elimination of suffering, it would be justifiable. A contrasting approach would be to hold that the destruction of human embryos falls under the widely accepted norm that forbids the intentional killing of innocent human beings, a norm that could be brought under the principle that requires us to do no harm: the principle of nonmaleficence.

These approaches suggest that the norms of common morality can be (perhaps always ought to be) justified from the perspective of principles such as the principle of beneficence and nonmaleficence. But since both of these approaches ascend to principles that seem to be equally compelling, how can one decide, in the case of research that destroys human embryos, which approach to embrace and which to reject? This leads us to an examination of first moral principles.

Notes

1. For an explanation of stem cells, their methods of procurement, and their potential uses, see President's Council on Bioethics (2002), chap. 4. See also President's Council "New Developments in Stem Cell Research," President's Council on Bioethics, https://bioethicsarchive.georgetown.edu/pcbe/topics/stemcells_in dex.html.

2. "Failure in vigilance, commitment, inclusiveness, or detachment is not immoral. It is simply foolish in the overall enterprise of living one's life.... *A human action ceases to be only imprudent and becomes also immoral when a specifiable instance of a human good is seriously affected (i.e., when there is harm involved).* This can happen through negligent failure to act; a positive, intentional action; or, more generally, unequal treatment." Gómez-Lobo (2002, 43–44; emphasis original).

3. Aquinas, S. Th. I-II. qq. 94–95; For acceptance of the idea of a "common morality" by two leading contemporary bioethicists see Beauchamp and Childress (2013, 410–29).

4. "Female genital mutilation (FGM) includes procedures that intentionally alter or cause injury to the female genital organs for non-medical reasons." World Health Organization (2014).

"the capacity for interests"—that is, those who lack awareness—cannot be harmed or wronged (Glannon 2005, 78). But whether harm requires awareness on the part of the subject is a substantial issue that should not be settled by invoking a notoriously ambiguous term like "interests." An adequate definition of "harm" must not depend on whether or not there is a drive toward a goal that would be thwarted by the harmful intervention. Stealing jewels from a woman who never wears them may not thwart any of her desires, but the theft surely inflicts financial harm. Raping a woman who is unconscious, whether temporarily or permanently, surely harms and wrongs her.

In natural law thinking, to harm someone is to deprive that person of a good. The greater the importance of the good, the greater the magnitude of the harm inflicted. Harm, which can be caused intentionally or unintentionally, constitutes an objective condition of which the person harmed may or may not be aware. It is perfectly possible for a patient to suffer harm while in a coma (if a wound is inflicted or if the patient is raped) or before full consciousness is achieved (if an unborn child is presently harmed by the mother's addiction to crack cocaine). It is also possible, on the other hand, to suffer pain without being harmed. If a physician in the course of a prescribed treatment causes pain, we do not judge that she is harming the patient. The pain may be caused, for example, by an injection in the leg that does not entail the loss of the function of the leg (and that may indeed save the function of the leg). Having a functioning limb is good for any person. But even if a surgeon amputates a gangrenous leg, she should not be accused of inflicting harm on the patient. The deprivation in this case is part of a broader concern for the whole body. The action is performed in pursuit of the good of the overall health of the patient. If the life and health of the patient can only be saved by amputation of a suppurating, gangrenous leg, amputation is not a harm. It is a benefit, indeed a vital benefit.

Moreover, the principle of nonmaleficence is respected in our examples of injection and of amputation not only because there is no deprivation of a good but also because there is no intention on the part of the physician to deprive the patient of a good. Natural law thinkers use the word "intention" in its ordinary sense of "aim" or "purpose." To intend a goal entails aiming to bring about an effect (in this case, a harm) and a decision to bring the effect about by effective means. Neither of these two conditions is met in our two examples.

There are cases in which a physician may produce harm unintentionally, if, for example, during the course of a complex surgical procedure, a blood vessel is punctured or a nerve severed. The unintended harm may or may not be due to negligence, but both alternatives—namely, negligent and nonnegligent conduct (and whether involving an action or an omission)—are better understood as a failure in the protection of a good rather than as the infliction of harm. The same holds true for actions that involve risks of harm. All such cases of unintended harm are to be understood primarily as violations of beneficence, for violations of nonmaleficence, in the strict sense, require intentionally depriving someone of a good.

Let us now return to the lab and the question we posed at the start of the previous chapter, whether it is ethical for Stella to disaggregate the six human embryos in vitro. We now have a better view of the moral conflict involved. One side (position A) argues that by not proceeding with the extraction of the stem cells, Stella is violating the moral principle of beneficence. Although it may not be her intention, she is depriving future patients of the good of health since their health could (let us assume) be restored by treatments derived from embryonic stem cell research. The other side (position B) holds that by destroying the human embryos, Stella is in violation of the moral principle of nonmaleficence because she is intentionally depriving those embryos of the good of life. Since life is a basic good (and one that plays a foundational role without which we cannot enjoy any other good), it follows that deliberately destroying the embryos amounts to inflicting the most serious form of harm possible.

Although we have not yet managed to resolve the initial question about the morality of embryo destruction, we have made some progress on two fronts. On the one hand, we have a better view of how the opposing views should be articulated. Each invokes a different moral principle to justify its conclusion. So we seem to be facing not simply a dispute about a particular case but apparently a conflict between general moral principles. On the other hand, our discussion of the first moral principles has naturally led us to identify certain basic goods by reference to which beneficence and nonmaleficence make sense and acquire their rationale. The foundational goods we have noticed so far are health and life. The deprivations that constitute the corresponding forms of harm are illness and death.

Life (in its most basic biological sense) and health (in all its functional complexity) are certainly not the only "basic" human goods—goods, that is, that are ends in themselves and not merely instrumentally good, as means to another good. Having family and friends, being knowledgeable, and appreciating art and beauty are also basic goods that make for a truly flourishing human life. (And basic goods are self-evidently good for us. If someone argued that death, disease, loneliness, ignorance, philistinism, etc., were good for us, or asked for reasons why health, friendship, knowledge, etc., were good, we might reasonably begin to wonder whether they had parted company with reality.) All the basic goods are equally basic: there is in this respect no hierarchy among them. But in the context of bioethics, life and health are the key, relevant basic goods. Life and health are not only good in themselves, they are good instrumentally as well, enabling us to participate in the other goods.

If we all agree in principle that it is rational and morally obligatory to pursue health and to preserve human life, why is there such disagreement surrounding the ethics of research on human embryos?

Note

The discussion in this book of the natural law understanding of the principles of nonmaleficence, beneficence, and justice should be read in the light of the discussion of the guidelines of "respect," "care," and "impartiality" in Gómez-Lobo (2002), chap. 4.

Chapter 3
THE ETHICAL DIVIDE

There are several reasons why disputes in bioethics, such as the dispute about research on human embryos, can be so difficult to resolve. Prominent among them is the lack of agreement on certain basic philosophical matters such as the interpretation of the moral principles and the so-called moral status of human beings of a certain age and condition. The former are issues in ethics, the latter in ontology.

One of the main disagreements in ethics today concerns the focus of the moral judgment. When we bring an action under a norm or directly under a principle in order to assess its morality, should we concentrate on the action's consequences, or should we consider primarily the action itself?

The doctrine that the morality of an action should be decided exclusively by reference to its consequences is aptly called consequentialism. Together with hedonism (the claim that pleasure is the one intrinsic good) and majoritism (the claim that the morally right action is the one that aims at the greatest good of the greatest number), consequentialism is one of the defining characteristics of classical utilitarianism, a moral theory commonly invoked today in bioethics.[1] At its core is the notion that the right course of action is that which produces the greatest good for the greatest number, "good" often being conceived in terms of pleasure. The master principle for the utilitarian is to produce the greatest pleasure for the greatest number.[2] The standard utilitarian argument in favor of embryonic stem cell research, reflected in what we called position A, interprets the principle of beneficence in consequentialist terms and justifies embryo research by appeal to the expectation that many people will be cured of a range of illnesses. The state of affairs thus achieved would be one in which pain has been minimized and pleasure maximized.

Other philosophers, however, are nonconsequentialists. They reject the claim that the morality of an action should be decided on the basis of consequences and consequences alone. A plausible objection to consequentialism may be introduced along the following lines. Imagine a car accident in which the driver, Stan, is severely injured but has a very good chance of survival. A team of paramedics arrives on the scene. They consider the overall ethical situation, including the acute shortage in their hospital of organs for transplantation. They decide against providing emergency treatment to Stan so that he will die and his organs used to save lives of patients in their hospital. Denied the emergency treatment he needs, Stan duly dies and his organs are later successfully transplanted into five seriously ill patients who would otherwise have died.

In judging the paramedics' omission to save Stan, it seems clear that they did not violate the principle of nonmaleficence. They did not cause the accident, nor did they intentionally worsen Stan's condition. Their action seemed to follow the principle of beneficence, at least under the strict consequentialist interpretation, for they aimed at maximizing the overall good, the greatest good for the greatest number. One life was lost, but five were saved. And yet any reasonable observer will surely grant that the paramedics acted wrongly.

Under what principle can we justify the conclusion that they acted wrongly? The omission was a failure to care for the victim and, as such, a failure in beneficence. But why should one care for only one individual instead of caring for a larger number? Shouldn't one be guided by the anticipated benefit for the majority? The correct reply will require us to mention a novel element: the omission that led to the death of the victim not only resulted in harm (Stan lost the good of life), but Stan was also wronged. It was unfair to him to omit due treatment in order to use his organs for others. We could even say that Stan had a right to be treated as victims of car accidents ought to be treated, that is, with a view to their own welfare and not primarily to the welfare of others.

To claim that someone was wronged, that he or she had a right, and that there was unequal and unfair treatment is to introduce the concept of justice into the debate. Although we are used to making claims of justice and fairness in different contexts of our lives, it is notoriously difficult to formulate a general notion of justice and to specify the criteria that determine just actions and fair distributions. Since our present purpose is to object to the consequentialist interpretation of the first moral principles, it is sufficient at this point to rely on our ordinary conviction that certain things are due or owed to certain persons, and that what is due or owed should not be omitted or withheld simply because there is an alternative that promises to bring about better overall results. Indeed, the principle of justice, in its broadest formulation, commands that every agent should give others what is due or owed to them, without further qualification. This is not to say, for example, that accident victims have a right to whatever treatment could help them. Resources are not unlimited, and doctors often face difficult moral decisions about how best to allocate scarce resources. But our example did not concern such a case. The paramedics had the resources to save Stan: they simply chose not to use them. Our example concerned the unjust deprivation of a patient's own vital organs in order to help other patients.

Many other similar examples of unjust treatment of an individual in order to maximize overall good could be given, and can be found in the ethical literature. If a town's police chief lynches an innocent black person in order to pacify racist rioters, has he acted ethically because the rioters would otherwise have burned the town to the ground and there was no other way to stop them? If hospital orderlies rape a patient who is and will remain unaware of the rape, such as a patient in a permanent coma, have they acted ethically because it gives them pleasure and causes her no discomfort? If a doctor researches on a competent patient without her consent—or even against her wishes—while she is temporarily unconscious, has the doctor acted ethically if the research makes an important advance in medical science? If a doctor cuts off a Somalian woman's clitoris, has the doctor acted ethically if the woman freely requested it because it is standard practice in her culture?

Anyone who admits that there are binding requirements of justice, and that certain acts (and omissions) are inherently unjust, will have to abandon the consequentialist interpretation of beneficence. Consequences are, to be sure, an important aspect of ethical judgment. It is prudent and right, for example, to use medical resources responsibly, to maximize the benefit they can produce. It is wasteful and wrong to use them irresponsibly, to save five lives when they could without unfairness have saved ten. But it is not always the case that the morality of an action is determined exclusively by its consequences. If the action itself is unjust, it would be morally wrong to perform it even if it were conducive to the greatest pleasure or happiness of the greatest number (whatever that means and however it is to be calculated, assuming it could be calculated at all).

Within the consequentialist camp, however, some utilitarians have introduced the distinction between "act" and "rule" utilitarianism in order to avoid the unpalatable approval of an obvious injustice. According to act utilitarianism, an action should be judged by reference to its expected consequences. According to rule utilitarianism, an action should be judged by reference to a rule that in turn should be judged by reference to the consequences of general compliance with the rule. Upholders of this second alternative can hold that, generally, decisions to provide due care to the victim of an accident bring about better social results than decisions based on the particular calculations in any individual case. However, in order to remain in the consequentialist camp, they must take the rule as merely provisional, as a rule of thumb, that may (or should) be violated when the evidence of maximization of benefit is particularly strong.

To those in the nonconsequentialist camp, such as natural law ethicists, treating others justly is not a matter of maximizing pleasure or happiness. Indeed, treating others justly sometimes requires choosing against huge anticipated benefits. There are some things (like rape or torture or the intentional killing of the innocent) that should never be done, however much pleasure or happiness for the majority they would produce.

The criticism of consequentialism hitherto has focused on one of its key defects: its injunction that we endorse whatever will maximize overall pleasure (or other such "utile" supposed to be maximizable). That is indeed a serious defect. But it is by no means its only defect. We should mention, if only in passing, a number of others. First, there is the practical difficulty of predicting consequences, especially in the medium to long-term future. Even meteorologists, aided by the latest satellite technology, regularly fail accurately to predict tomorrow's weather. It is often much more difficult to predict the consequences of human conduct (including the reactions of other people, and the effects of one's conduct upon oneself). Second, there is the difficulty of "weighing" the consequences to determine the overall good. For example, which will produce the greatest pleasure for the greatest number: giving money to subsidize concerts at Carnegie Hall, or to build a hospice in Harlem, or to endow a Chair at Oxford University, or to subsidize "happy hours" in Boston bars? Finally, is "pleasure" (or other such "utile" considered similarly quantifiable) really the ultimate or sole intrinsic good to which we should direct our efforts? Might some people not derive great pleasure from things any reasonable observer knows to be wrong (such as rape)?[3]

What characterizes, then, a nonconsequentialist interpretation of beneficence in the natural law tradition? First, it would be seriously wrong to think that whereas consequentialism attaches importance to consequences, natural law does not. Nothing could be further from the truth. It is obviously irresponsible to overlook the consequences of one's proposed acts or omissions. Consequences matter. Take Brad. He is an abusive parent who repeatedly beats his child, Zak, with a baseball bat. Brad brings about a terrible consequence: the infliction of serious physical and emotional harm on Zak. Conversely, Kelly is a responsible parent who ensures that her daughter, Mary, is loved and well cared for. Kelly brings about a very good consequence: a child who is physically and emotionally healthy. So natural law ethics takes very seriously indeed the consequences of conduct and whether conduct promotes or impedes human flourishing or participation in the basic goods. What natural law theory rejects is the claim that the moral evaluation of our conduct should be based *solely* on its expected consequences. On the natural law view, the focus is on how the goods protected by morality fare both in the consequences and in the action itself. In short, it is a both/and, not an either/or, approach to morality.

In our earlier example of the car accident, regard for the well-being of Stan, as required by the nonconsequentialist, natural law interpretation of beneficence, coincides with justice. In fact, the normative principle of justice that requires us to give each person his or her due is a specific application of the general principle of beneficence. It adds to the general requirement of care for the good of others (and for our own good) the further precision that in a subset of cases care for the good is due or owed. We are not forced to choose between what is good and what is just: they go hand in hand.

The nonconsequentialist approach avoids the conflict between the principle of beneficence and the principle of justice because it does not posit a future state of affairs called "social utility," characterized as the greatest pleasure or happiness for the greatest number. In contrast with that approach, care for the collective good has been traditionally formulated by natural law ethics in terms of "the common good." This good encompasses all of the conditions that allow members of the human community successfully to engage in the pursuit of their own goods, their own flourishing. Viewed in this comprehensive way, the common good does not exclude but rather includes respect for justice, for unfair dealings are a major obstacle to people seeking their own flourishing. Violating Stan's rights, the right to be stabilized and taken to hospital, violates the common good in spite of the utilitarian benefit rendered to the five recipients of his organs. In short, the common good includes and respects individual rights and holds that individuals should not be treated unjustly, even if unjust treatment would benefit a majority.

Someone might object that on certain occasions the individual good has to yield to the good of the majority, for example, when the expropriation of private land is necessary to allow the building of a public road, hospital, or school for the benefit of the many. This is true, but rights to land are not absolute, unlike basic human rights—such as the right not to be intentionally killed, enslaved, tortured, or raped—which are absolute. Indeed, property law, like the criminal law, exists to safeguard not only the good of the individual but also the good of the community. Rape is an unjust violation of not only the rights of an individual, but of the good of the community. This explains why criminals are prosecuted and punished in the name of the community ("the State," "the People," or "the Crown"), and not by the victim or the victim's relatives. Criminal punishment is retribution, not vengeance, and is meted out according to the requirements of justice, according to what is due to the criminal, what the criminal deserves.[4] This is why we talk of our system of criminal *justice*. So, too, property law is shot through with concern for the common good. The rights of the owner of property are not absolute. There are many rightful restrictions on how owners of land (or cars or guns) may use their property, and sometimes the community is entitled even to deprive the owner of his or her land, for public use (the law of "eminent domain" or "compulsory purchase").[5] Of course, the expropriation must be justified: it is one thing to expropriate property because it is needed to build a much-needed public hospital, but quite another to do so to build a holiday home for the mayor's mistress. Moreover, appropriate compensation should be paid to the property owner: it would be unjust simply to seize the land without compensation. The principle at stake here is the very same one as in the accident case involving Stan: no human being should be treated as a mere means to further the goals of others.

Historically, there has been at least one egregious practice that obviously involves treating human beings as mere means "for the sake of another": slavery. In the historical opposition to slavery we have come to emphasize freedom, its direct opposite. Respect for the freedom of human beings is a requirement of justice. It is unfair not to allow a person to live "for her own sake," that is, in pursuit of his or her own goods as he or she sees fit. On the other hand, freedom cannot and should not be exercised in a totally unrestricted manner. The limits imposed on the exercise of freedom are also requirements of justice. If my action violates someone else's right to some good, then it would be morally wrong for me to perform it. As the saying goes, my right to swing my fist ends at the point of your nose.[6] Ultimately, however, the restriction of freedom rests on nonmaleficence. A free choice that intentionally harms someone is morally unacceptable. It is also morally unacceptable intentionally to harm oneself, as by selling oneself into slavery, undergoing female genital mutilation, having a healthy limb amputated, using crack cocaine, agreeing to be killed and eaten, or killing oneself.

Freedom enters the contemporary bioethical debate in the language of "autonomy." According to some authors, this notion adds to freedom of choice the idea of a freely adopted plan. On this assumption, autonomy is a much stronger condition for action than freedom. A patient may freely accept or reject a treatment proposed by her physician, but a truly autonomous patient would decide as part of an overarching project or clear design concerning her treatment. The implausibility of the latter condition (unless the patient is herself a physician) leads most authors to use the term "autonomous action" in a way that makes it equivalent simply to "voluntary" or "freely chosen action," regardless of whether the agent makes the choice in light of a broad plan. In what follows, an "autonomous" choice means a free and informed choice. The moral "principle of autonomy" can be formulated as follows: every agent should respect the freely chosen actions of a person as long as they do not harm others.

The claims that autonomy should be respected, that patients should not be treated without their freely chosen and informed consent, and that interventions should not be imposed on unwilling patients are requirements of justice. We owe it to people—certain emergencies aside—to step back and allow them to pursue their own plan for participation in the basic goods, as they see fit. There are many different choices consistent with true human well-being, and different patients may well have different priorities in their pursuit of the basic goods. Take just one hypothetical scenario, concerning Nora and Nigel. Nora is retired and spends much of her time at home with her kittens, knitting. Nigel plays football for Notre Dame University, loves the sport, and hopes to become a professional footballer. They both have back pain. The surgeon explains to each of them that she can perform an operation to relieve the pain, but that the procedure involves a one-in-a-thousand risk of paralysis in the right leg. Nora and Nigel are confronted with the same operation and the same risk of paralysis as a side effect, but they may arrive at different decisions about whether to consent to the operation. The risk of paralysis may assume far less importance in Nora's decision making than it does in Nigel's. Paralysis for Nigel would dash his hopes of a future career in football. Nigel refuses the operation, but it would be unreasonable to say his decision was mistaken, let alone unethical.[7]

Even when a decision is based on a patient's obviously mistaken understanding of the facts, it does not follow that the physician may override a patient's autonomous refusal. If a patient, Lucy, whose prognosis is good refuses a treatment on the grounds that she thinks it will be ineffective, her attending physician can judge that she is making a mistake with regard to the pursuit of the good involved—namely, her health, or perhaps even life itself. He should try to correct her misunderstanding about the effectiveness of the procedure. But if, at the end of the day, Lucy does not change her mind, he should respect her decision and withhold the procedure because the patient—indeed, every human person—should act in light of what she sees as the good to be pursued and the evil to be avoided. Not to do so would be for her to act against her particular judgment about the situation at hand. It would be to act against the dictates of her moral conscience. Respect for the autonomous choices of patients is thus grounded on respect for their conscience, the human power that provides the ultimate and irreplaceable guide for action.

But does respect for autonomous choice require a physician to comply with every autonomous decision of a patient? This question has arisen acutely in relation to abortion. Is a physician, Dr. Morgan, who regards abortion as the killing of an innocent human being, under an ethical duty to grant a woman's request for an abortion, or at least to refer her to a physician willing to perform an abortion? Following the principle identified above, it seems clear that Dr. Morgan should do neither. In fact, a physician has to be guided by her own conscience so that if she is asked to perform an action by which, in her judgment, she would impair or destroy an instance of a basic human good, she should refuse. Respect for autonomous choices of a patient that do not harm others does not require compliance with autonomous requests to produce harm to the patient herself even though the patient may in good faith see it not as harm but as benefit. Respect for autonomy is, properly understood, more like a shield than a sword. It is one thing for a patient to refuse the offer of an operation or drugs and for a physician to respect that refusal. It is quite another for a patient to demand an operation or drugs and expect the physician to comply with that demand. The principle of conscience can be formulated as follows: every agent should perform an action only if she judges it to be morally permissible, and should refrain from performing it if she judges it to be morally impermissible. Since the principle of autonomy only tells us that we should respect autonomous choices that do not harm others, but does not tell us anything about the morality of those choices, it follows that a judgment of conscience does not need to yield to the autonomy of someone else. A conscientious agent may in fact judge that an important human good of that person herself is being attacked in her autonomously chosen action and that it would therefore be both irrational and immoral to yield and cooperate. If, for example, helping patients to kill themselves is unethical, and a patient, Gary, asks his doctor, Dr. Mitchell, for a lethal prescription, Dr. Mitchell should conscientiously refuse his request, however autonomous it may be.[8]

Standardly, physicians do not see themselves merely as technicians to prescribe whatever drugs or perform whatever operations are requested by patients, however autonomous those requests may be. And rightly so. A physician (or other professional, whether teacher, minister of religion, or lawyer) should always put the true good of the patient (student, believer, client) first, and not simply do whatever they are asked to do.[9] Sadly, this understanding of professionalism is under increasing threat in modern society. Some doctors seem to be little more than scalpels and prescription pads for hire.

In general, the principle of autonomy rightly requires physicians to respect the free and informed choices of patients. Natural law ethics holds that the person primarily responsible for the health of the patient is the patient, not the physician (though the patient ought to seek medical advice whenever that is required to help her safeguard her health). But natural law ethics avoids the extreme and untenable position that respect for patient choice should be unlimited. The reader of the contemporary bioethical literature could be forgiven for thinking that much of contemporary bioethics adopts, or at least seems to adopt, something like this extreme version of the principle of respect for autonomy. This may well be because much of contemporary bioethics appears to lack any substantive conception of what is truly good for human beings and therefore falls back onto respect for the autonomous choices that patients happen to make. Respect for autonomy too often seems to serve as a bioethical default position. This could help to account for the contemporary emphasis on the right to choose rather than on the rightness of the choice made. But a little reflection is (or should be) sufficient to show that respect for choice cannot sensibly be unlimited. For example, it is often claimed, in articles on bioethics and biomedical law, that the right of competent patients to refuse treatment is absolute. But even respect for refusals of treatment by patients, what might be called the Holy of Holies of Autonomy, cannot sensibly be unlimited. Let us consider just one example.

Sarah visits Dr. Semmelweis, complaining of a fever. Sarah tests positive for a highly infectious and deadly virus, as deadly as Ebola but even more likely to spread though the community. Dr. Semmelweis tells her she must be quarantined and undergo treatment to stop its spread. Sarah, who is completely competent, refuses. She insists on going back to her house where she mistakenly thinks she will get better, or at least be no risk to others. Dr. Semmelweis contacts the local public health officials. When the officials arrive, Sarah adamantly refuses to go with them. "I am an autonomous woman," she shouts. "You have no right to touch me without my consent." She sits down and refuses to budge. The officials remove her, over her strident vocal protests, to the isolation ward of a local hospital. Sarah repeatedly tries to leave the ward, pushing past the nurses. The physicians order the use of restraining straps as the least restrictive means of confining her to her room. Was Sarah treated unethically? Of course not: Sarah's conduct endangered the community. So even the right to refuse treatment cannot be absolute.

Now that we have introduced and offered a natural law interpretation of a certain number of principles (nonmaleficence, beneficence, justice, autonomy, and conscience) we may return to our initial moral

problem. How do these principles equip us to judge the ethics of research on human embryos in vitro?

Surely Stella must follow her conscience regarding researching on
the embryos. She goes wrong if she fails to do what her conscience tells
her is right, but this does not mean that her judgment of conscience is
infallible and that she acts rightly whenever she follows her conscience.
It can go wrong—and when it does, she acts wrongly both when she
fails to follow and when she follows it—and because of this it is not
a purely private or subjective affair. The judgment of conscience is a
public matter in the sense that we can require Stella to justify her judgment. We often inquire whether our own judgment is true, and try to
show to others it is true, and inquire of others whether their judgment
is true, and try to show them that their judgment is or is not true. We
remonstrate with the racist or sexist, or with someone bent on doing
something she regards as permissible if we have good reason to think it
is not. Would we not—should we not—try to dissuade someone who
told us they were going to join a terrorist organization and plant bombs
on passenger planes, however conscientiously they had arrived at their
decision? Hence, even if the claim that Stella is following her conscience
leads us to refrain from assigning her personal guilt, it does not solve the
problem of deciding whether in researching on the embryos she will be
acting morally or immorally.

The fact that Stella is acting autonomously does not resolve the issue
either. The principle of respect for autonomy only requires a second
party not to interfere with autonomous actions (and even then we saw
it is not unlimited: sometimes we may—indeed, ought to—interfere
with autonomous actions), but it does not contribute to the discernment of the morality of the autonomous action itself. A perfectly autonomous choice may be morally wrong.

So we are led back to the first moral principles, that is, to nonmaleficence and beneficence. Insofar as the purely consequentialist interpretation of beneficence has been rejected, we have moved forward on one
front: the expected results of embryo experimentation are not, as position A holds, sufficient by themselves to justify embryo destruction. We
have to consider how the relevant human goods fare in the action itself,
as position B enjoins us to do. If there is also unfairness involved, then
the action may entail violations of both nonmaleficence and justice.

At this point the objection can be raised that, in the case of an adult, intentional dismemberment to provide organs for others would be both an extreme form of harm and a monstrous injustice but that in the case of embryos there is neither harm nor injustice. Human embryos, it is argued, cannot be harmed nor can they be treated unfairly. They are, it might even be argued, just "a clump of cells." We must now, therefore, turn from ethics to ontology. What is a human embryo: a person, or a thing, or something else?

Notes

1. For arguments for and against utilitarianism, see Smart and Williams (1973).

2. There are varieties of consequentialism. Some consequentialists regard the good to be maximized as "happiness" or "preferences" rather than "pleasure." However, consequentialists agree that ethics is about maximizing the good, and that maximization justifies whatever means are required. One of the best known utilitarian ethicists is Peter Singer. See, for example, Singer (1996, 2011).

3. For criticisms of consequentialism see, for example, Finnis (1983); Fitzpatrick (1988, chap. 5); Gómez-Lobo (2002), 113–19; and Oderberg (2000a, 2000b; Oderberg and Laing 1997).

4. For a natural law view of punishment, see Bradley (2003). As this illustrates, the system of criminal justice, like Western professional medical ethics, has been largely informed by natural law thinking.

5. See Gray and Gray (2009, pt. 11).

6. For a natural law perspective on when it is legitimate for the criminal law to restrict human freedom, see George (1995).

7. For Dr. Pellegrino's analysis of the good of the patient see Pellegrino and Thomasma (1988).

8. On the right to conscientious objection, see generally Kaczor (2013, chaps. 12 and 13).

9. On the role and responsibilities of physicians, see Pellegrino and Thomasma (1988, 1993).

Chapter 4

THE ONTOLOGICAL DIVIDE

In contemporary bioethics there is not only a dispute between consequentialist and nonconsequentialist interpretations of the moral principles. There is also a deep controversy about who or what human embryos are. This controversy concerns our whole understanding of ourselves.

As we noted earlier, the term "ontology" has been borrowed from the Aristotelian tradition and is the discipline concerned with "knowledge of *being*"—that is, with identifying the nature of things, what kind of *being* they are. Ethics, on the other hand, is the discipline that studies which human actions ought to be performed and which ought not to be performed. Ontology is a vast field covering many interesting questions, but here we shall restrict ourselves to questions that have a direct bearing on contemporary bioethics. Our strategy will be eminently Socratic. We start out from a claim linking ethics and ontology about which the different parties to the debate are in agreement and then move forward from that agreement to the disputed issues.

In contemporary debates there is general agreement that it is wrong intentionally to harm normal human adults. This agreement involves an ontological claim about the nature of normal human adults and an ethical claim about how one ought to treat them. This twofold agreement can be expressed in various ways. One of the favored formulations has been that human adults are endowed with a set of properties that make them persons and that persons should be treated in a certain manner. Indeed, to be a person, it has been traditionally assumed, is to be endowed with dignity, and to have dignity is to be different from, and superior to, mere things that may be instrumentalized. The dignity of persons requires us to treat them as ends in themselves.

According to the philosopher Immanuel Kant and earlier philosophical tradition, "dignity" expresses the value of persons whereas "price" expresses the value of things (Kant [2012], 4:434–35).[1] Although there can be variations in price, dignity does not admit of variations or degrees. A being either has dignity or it does not. Some contemporary philosophers have introduced the terms "moral status" and "moral standing" to play a role more or less similar to that of "dignity." Moral status, in their view, protects its possessor from being destroyed insofar as it gives him or her a claim on others: the claim to be respected. But moral status is conceived by many authors as ranging from "full" moral status to lesser degrees of moral status. And the variations are taken to occur not only among classes (e.g., mice having a lower moral status than human adults), but also among stages of the same individual. For example, a fetus has a higher moral status than an embryo, and an adult more than a fetus. Whether it is sensible to replace the notion of dignity with that of moral status is something we shall critically assess after we have attempted to clarify the foundation upon which both dignity and "full moral status" are alleged to rest: "personhood."

It is important to note that the word "person" as employed in bioethics (and in ethics generally) can have both a descriptive meaning and a prescriptive meaning: it can not only describe the being but can also indicate how we ought to treat it. For an auctioneer to call a painting "an excellent painting" is both to say something about it and to encourage bidding. Likewise, "person" is often used not only to describe an individual but also to issue an injunction about how to treat her. In fact, the description provides (implicitly) the reasons for the prescription. To fail to attend to these two different meanings of the "person" creates confusion (Veatch 2012, 29–30).

The properties that comprise personhood in the descriptive sense can be presented as a list of capacities for certain activities, such as the exercise of consciousness and self-consciousness, of reasoning (both practical and theoretical), and of freedom to choose and moral agency. The list can be drawn up in different ways. What is important is to realize that the human capacities or powers that make us persons are tightly interrelated. For example, freedom to choose is related to the exercise of reason, and moral agency is connected to self-consciousness. You cannot have one without the other. In earlier philosophical tradition these properties were summed up in the Aristotelian formula "having *lógos*" or, in a broad sense, being rational.[2] Only a physician aware of what she is doing, having engaged in professional and prudential deliberation, can freely choose to heal or to kill a patient. Such is the power of persons. Neither fire nor foxes can act in this manner. Fire cannot but burn. Foxes cannot choose between healing or killing their prey (ask in any hen house).

It is clear that both ancient and contemporary characterizations of persons take their cue from normal human adults, those humans who can exercise immediately and at will the relevant mental capacities. Some even call adults "paradigmatic persons" and ask, for example, whether infants, fetuses, and embryos, or certain higher animals, are close enough to this paradigm to qualify as persons. The primary focus on human adults has in turn generated a perplexity in the use of the term "person," which may be responsible for some of the disagreements. Let us take a closer look.

Some terms express what sort of thing an object is; others express what stage of development a thing is at.[3] Take the word "puppy." When a puppy grows up, it ceases to be a puppy, it does not cease to exist, and we say accordingly that "puppy" is a term used to characterize a dog during a particular phase of its life. But when a dog dies, it ceases to be a dog, and what is left is a decomposing body, a corpse. We say accordingly that "dog" is a term that expresses what an object essentially is such that when it ceases to be a thing of that sort, it ceases to exist. This characterization equally holds for the coming-into-being of an object.

The distinction between these two sorts of terms, between, on the one hand, nature or kind and, on the other, phase of development, tracks two further distinctions. If an object undergoes a change in one of its properties, and if the property lost or acquired is essential to what it is, the object becomes something different from what it was. We then speak of a "substantial" change.[4] There are two kinds of substantial change: coming-to-be and ceasing-to-be. On the other hand, when the property lost or acquired relates to a stage of development of a thing, the object becomes different but not *something* different. An adult dog is different from a puppy, but it is the same dog, which has now reached a mature stage in its life. The change in this case is what is called an "accidental" change.[5] In contrast with coming-to-be and ceasing-to-be, between generation and corruption, this kind of change is merely an alteration. We shall call an object that comes to be a "substance," and we shall call a property that a substance acquires due to an alteration an "accident." Thus, a dog is a "substance" while the property of its now being at the puppy stage is an "accident."

When some people—notably, upholders of position A (those in favor of destructive human embryo research)—allude to "a fetus becoming a person," they are referring to a specific organism (a fetus) that takes on a set of new properties (the ones associated with personhood, such as self-consciousness). A close parallel is the talk about "a child becoming a teenager." Since in these instances the fetus and the child do not cease to exist, it is reasonable to assume that both terms, "person" and "teenager," are being used to refer to stages of development. But it is surely a mistake to confuse what a thing is with its stage of development and to say, "This is not a person: it is a teenager (or an embryo)." Becoming a person is drastically different from becoming a teenager. When a person comes to be, something completely new begins to exist, and this obviously is not the case when one becomes a teenager.

Some of those opposed to destructive research on embryos and who espouse position B claim that a fetus or an embryo is already a person. This seems so obviously false to some of those who espouse position A that they barely take time to refute it. Those who do try to refute it usually call attention to the properties a person has and an embryo lacks. A person can think, talk, feel, act, choose; an embryo cannot. Therefore, they conclude, it is mistaken, if not absurd, to claim that an embryo is a person. But, they are using the word "person" to refer to a particular stage of development: the adult stage of a normal human being. And an embryo, obviously, is not an adult.

When some of those who espouse position B claim that an embryo is a person, they take "person" to refer not to an advanced stage of development, the adult stage, but (in line with earlier philosophical tradition) to the type of being the embryo is, a being that has the capacity for rational thought, free choice, and moral agency, even if it is unable to exercise that capacity until a more mature stage of its development.

This does not mean that adherents of position B are using the term "person" simply to mean "human being" but rather for an essential property of humankind. This is a property every human possesses in so far as he or she is human: the capacity for rational thought, free choice and moral agency. Whether there might be other beings in the universe endowed with this capacity is thereby left open.[6]

The claim that personhood is an essential property of human beings is logically equivalent to the thesis that rationality is so deeply embedded in our nature that we come to be as rational beings and that we cease to exist when we cease to be rational beings. But isn't this precisely what adherents of position A hold, namely, that we begin to exist when we begin to think or at least to exercise consciousness, and that we cease to exist when we lose consciousness or the use of our minds, something that may occur long before our biological death? Isn't a person a being that is always preceded, and sometimes followed, by an organism different from it?

These difficulties bring us to the heart of the matter. How we ought to treat human embryos is a function of how we understand ourselves as adults, since we all agree that normal human adults such as those reading this book should be respected in the specific sense that they should not be intentionally killed or destroyed. Treatment of embryos is a function of how we understand ourselves now because this understanding determines our relationship to them. Is a human embryo a predecessor of a human adult that, precisely because a predecessor, does not require our respect in the same way as an adult? Or is a human embryo the same as a human adult, only younger, so that it deserves the same respect as an adult?

Underlying many contemporary bioethical disputes are two rival ontological conceptions of what we are. These conceptions are operative as foundational assumptions that determine much of what is built upon them, although for the most part they remain hidden from sight. The two conceptions can be characterized in broad outline as follows:

1. On the first view, which is often called the "dualist" view, the core of our being is our mind or consciousness.[7] The key intuition or self-evident claim behind this view is my awareness of myself. It is a "first-person singular" perspective. As long as I am conscious of the fact that I am thinking, I am assured that I exist, and if I should become permanently unconscious, the person that I am would no longer exist, even if my body continued to live. Indeed, my body is somehow external to me, for I am, on this view, what might be called a "nonbodily person," or a "mind inhabiting a body." When Jane watches her mother baking a cake in the kitchen, Jane does not see a person: she sees only a biological organism. The person is her mother's mind, which merely inhabits her body. If her mother develops advanced dementia, she ceases to be a person, and all that remains is a biological organism.

2. On the second and competing view, often called the "monist" view,

the core of our being is our life.[8] We are, on this conception, sentient living organisms endowed with mental properties, properties that we might cease to exercise without thereby ceasing to exist ourselves. This is a "first-person plural" perspective. Indeed, the root of this view is the common experience of interacting with other persons whom we see and identify primarily as bodily beings and whose bodies do not appear to us as external to who they are. When Jane watches her mother bake a cake, she sees her mother, not merely a biological organism. If her mother develops advanced dementia and Jane visits her in the nursing home, Jane still sees her mother and not merely a biological organism. We are, on this view, what might be called "personal bodies" or "a substantial unity of mind and body."[9]

Which of the two basic ontological views, the dualist or the monist, is correct? This has been vigorously disputed since antiquity, and there is an extensive literature from ancient Greece to the present day containing arguments on both sides. It would be an illusion to think that this question can be finally settled within the covers of this short book. But the book can offer a few lines of reasoning to suggest the implausibility of the first view and the plausibility of the second.[10]

A good starting point is the application of some of our earlier distinctions. If Sophie is a mind inhabiting a body, then a "substantial" change took place when Sophie's mind began to function. If so, then two generations must have taken place, first the generation of Sophie's body and then the generation of Sophie's mind. It is the latter that counts as *Sophie's* coming-to-be. Sophie is a composite of two substances: an initially "unoccupied" body and a mind that began to "occupy" it at some point (McMahan 1999, 83).

Alternatively, if, as the second view would have it, Sophie is a living body capable of mental activity, then the change that took place when Sophie's mind began to function was only the development of a latent capacity, a capacity that was present from Sophie's beginning as a living body. The onset of mental activity was merely an "accidental" change that did not result in the coming-to-be of a new substance. Sophie is just one substance, and she began to exist when her body began to exist. As John Finnis, a leading defender of this view, has written: "One's living body is intrinsic, not merely instrumental, to one's personal life. Each of us has a human life (not a vegetable life plus an animal life plus a personal life); when it is flourishing that life includes all one's vital functions including speech, deliberation and choice; when gravely impaired it lacks some of those functions without ceasing to be the life of the person so impaired" (Finnis 1993, 334). In deciding which of these two conceptions, the dualist or the monist, is more likely to be true, and which squares better with our understanding of ourselves, can the empirical evidence from contemporary biology help?

Most people would surely have trouble thinking of themselves as somehow distinct from their body. They experience themselves primarily as a single bodily being occupying a place in space and subject to the ravages of time. Illness affects *them*, not something they occupy, and it is on this assumption that they worry about their health and well-being. We are immediately affected by everything that happens to our body, such as the pain of a wound. All this could perhaps be explained within a dualist framework by postulating a sophisticated theory of the copresence of two substances in the same place. However, the more sophisticated the theory, the less persuasive it will probably be. What seems to count decisively against dualism, though, is the fact that the empirical evidence makes it highly unlikely that a substantial change occurs when the mind arises.

Although at present there is no adequate understanding of how the mind and the brain are related to each other, there is general agreement that a functioning human brain is at least a necessary condition for the operation of the human mind. But there is no empirical evidence to show that the activation of the brain marks a radical new beginning. The brain is formed gradually as required by the human genotype and is part of the unified overall development of the human organism under the guidance of the human genome. Indeed, the neural activity that may indicate the onset of sentience arises at some point during gestation, but the brain continues to develop well after birth. If these elementary biological facts are taken into account, it becomes clear that the metaphor of an "unoccupied organism" before the detectable activation of a crucial human organ, the brain, is highly misleading. It is much more plausible to hold that a succession of continuous alterations is taking place in an organism that does not thereby receive something external or extraneous to itself. A young human body, by its genetic constitution, is internally programmed as a unified whole to undergo the alterations that lead to the activation of the mind. It undergoes a dynamic, self-directed progression toward the full actualization of its indwelling capacity.

The dualist understanding of personhood also invites two other objections that we should briefly mention, which we might call the "episodic" and the "equality" objections. First, on the dualist account, personhood can come and go, and this can create real difficulties deciding who is and who is not a person. If a dualist holds that personhood begins with self-consciousness, then Alf started to be a person when he became self-conscious. But doesn't this mean that Alf stops being a person when he falls asleep, or into a temporary or reversible coma? The dualist might reply that Alf is still a person in either case because he has the potential for self-consciousness. But then why doesn't the unborn child's potential for self-consciousness qualify him or her as a person?

Second, on the dualist account of personhood, only some human beings qualify as persons. Others do not. This account rejects something that many people regard as essential to any civilized society: the fundamental equality of all human beings. How defensible, how civilized, is a criterion that excludes from personhood—and therefore from basic rights—millions of babies, both born and unborn, and millions of human adults with advanced dementia? And what of all those with profound learning disabilities? Are they, too, "nonpersons," mere "biological organisms"?

As we noted earlier, the interpretation of the genetic program (a scientific concept) as an instance of potentiality (a philosophical concept) provides a renewed opportunity to understand and attempt to resolve the ontological divide underlying much of contemporary bioethics. We shall continue our exploration of these important matters in the next chapter.

Notes

1. For a recent analysis by a natural law philosopher of dignity in the bioethical context, see Kaczor (2013). For a volume containing a variety of perspectives on dignity, see President's Council on Bioethics (2008).

2. Aristotle describes this as the activation of a *dúnamis metà lógou,* "a power endowed with *lógos,*" that is, with the ability to assert or deny the same propositional content. *Metaphysics* IX. 2. 1046a 36-b 28. Here is not the place for a deep exploration of Aristotle's analysis of the relationship between mind and body.

3. Some philosophers use the word "sortal" in this context. A "proper sortal" is a term that refers to what a thing is; "phase sortal" is a term that tells us what stage of development the thing is at.

4. Or an "identity-nonpreserving" change.

5. Or an "identity-preserving" change.

6. The natural law position is not, then, as is often mistakenly claimed by some of its critics, "speciesist." It does not value only human beings and value them simply because they are members of the species *homo sapiens*. It holds that any creature who has the radical capacity for reason, free choice, and moral agency has the innate dignity of personhood. If members of other species, like great apes, had this capacity, they would be persons. Similarly, if fictional characters like Master Yoda really existed, they too would be persons.

7. This is what might be called the "Neo-Cartesian" view, after the French philosopher René Descartes (1596–1650), who famously wrote, "I think, therefore I am." Descartes (1637).

8. This is what we might call the "Neo-Aristotelian" view, after the Greek philosopher Aristotle (384–322 BC).

9. Deliberately omitted from the foregoing characterization of two fundamental ontological conceptions is any reference to the nature of the mind. Actually, each is compatible with both a materialist and an immaterialist understanding of the human capacity for thought. It is well known that Descartes took the mind or "thinking thing" (*res cogitans*) to be strictly immaterial, but is also clear that many contemporary Neo-Cartesians are materialists who would not follow him along that path. Likewise, a Neo-Aristotelian can hold either that mental events are bodily events or that they are not reducible to bodily events. The reason for not taking a stand here on the nature of the mind is to set aside as many sources of disagreement as possible in order to work towards pivotal agreements from which to draw ethical conclusions.

10. For a comprehensive treatment, see Lee and George (2008).

Chapter 5
POTENTIALITY AND GENETICS

The dispute we considered in the previous chapter between the dualist and the monist views of our nature hinges in part on how we should understand the rise of mental activity and the potentiality that allows such an important change to take place. The ontological notion of potentiality was originally introduced by Aristotle to explain any kind of change. If something becomes an F, the explanation goes, it was capable of becoming an F. It was an F potentially. If something cannot become an F, it lacks the corresponding potentiality. We can thus state that a human embryo has the potentiality to become a human adult whereas a cat embryo lacks that natural potentiality. Indeed, according to current knowledge, the potentiality (or lack thereof) corresponds to the specific capabilities of the genome of an organism, and such capabilities can be empirically ascertained.

Any potentiality requires external conditions for its actualization, but the external conditions do not determine the nature of the potentiality itself. It has been possible to gestate in a cow a cloned mammal from a different species, and this provides decisive evidence in support of the claim that the genotype, and therefore the species of the calf that is born, depends on the nucleus of cells of the embryo, not on the sustaining environment. This scientific fact in turn allows us to reject the frequent conflation of potentiality with probability. Some bioethicists would deny that a human embryo in a glass dish has the potentiality to become an adult ("the potential to become a person" in their wording) if the decision has been made not to implant it (Guenin 2008, 29–31). But this really means that it has zero probability of further development because it is being denied the necessary external conditions for its survival. If it is a genetically well-formed embryo, it has the intrinsic properties that constitute the potentiality, regardless of the factual probabilities of that potentiality being actualized. A normal human teenager has the potentiality to become an adult but has zero probability of doing so if stranded on the moon without oxygen. Once the potentiality of an embryo is shown to reside in the genetic program that includes information leading to the rudiments of the organs that sustain the mind, the dualist position becomes less and less plausible as an ontological doctrine. At no time is an embryo or a fetus "unoccupied" because the potentiality that is continuous with its own actualization was present in it from the beginning. You were a person from your very beginning, at your conception.

To avoid the controversy surrounding the use of the word "person" in the bioethical context, however, let us use "human being." It has been claimed that a major argument against abortion (which has direct implications for the dispute about embryo research) rests on the potentiality of the unborn. The argument runs as follows:

First premise: It is wrong to kill a potential human being.

Second premise: A human fetus is a potential human being.

Conclusion: Therefore it is wrong to kill a human fetus.

This way of framing the argument against abortion is, however, weak. The main weakness resides in the mistaken application of the notion of potentiality in the second premise. A human embryo or fetus is not a potential human being but a human being with potential. As Patrick Steptoe and (later Nobel Laureate) Robert Edwards, the pioneers of IVF, wrote about their initial agreement to collaborate on IVF, their work would enable them "to examine a microscopic human being— one in its very earliest stages of development" (Edwards and Steptoe 1981, 83). The human embryo already *is* a "man" (*homo, anthropos*), a living member of the human species, fully actualizing the basic biological functions of nutrition, metabolism, homeostasis, growth, and so on. Were those functions not actualized, he or she would be dead. What is potential is the exercise of the functions of the mature organism, among them the higher mental capacities that will be activated in due course, if all goes well. Thus, the first premise with its allusion to potentiality becomes irrelevant. The pertinent moral rule required for a valid antiabortion argument is simply the unrestricted injunction that it is wrong intentionally to kill an innocent human being.

There are two further arguments against the personhood of the embryo related to the role of potentiality that are equally unpersuasive. One is crafted as a *reductio ad absurdum* to sever the connection between potentiality and due respect. The second seeks to rupture the identity that holds between an embryo and an adult of the human species. These arguments are, respectively, the "argument from potentiality of the gametes" and the "argument from twinning."

Potentiality of the Gametes

This argument (see Glannon 2005, 79; Mahowald 2004; Gómez-Lobo 2004a; 2005) takes roughly the following form. Just as a fertilized egg has "the potential" for further development and is thus said to deserve respect, likewise an unfertilized egg has "the potential" to develop into a human being and hence also deserves respect, and, as this is absurd (since eggs and sperm are mere body parts), it is equally absurd to hold that a fertilized egg should be respected.

This argument fails. Appeal to basic facts in genetics shows that the assumed "potential" of the unfertilized egg is utterly different from that of the fertilized egg. The absurdity of the interim conclusion does not require us to drop the initial premise. An unfertilized egg is a cell produced by division (meiosis) that only has half, twenty-three, of the normal full set of human chromosomes. Strictly speaking it is a unipotent cell, a cell that because of its genetic constitution has only one potentiality: the potentiality to fuse with a sperm to form a new organism. An unfertilized egg simply does not have within itself the genetic wherewithal to develop into a human being.

A fertilized egg on the other hand is no longer a gamete. Since it has the full complement of human chromosomes, comprising twenty-three from the egg and twenty-three from the sperm, the original egg has ceased to exist and has been replaced by a new organism that is already genetically human. This organism can indeed develop into an adult because it has within itself all of the genetic information required for its self-directed development. It is, unlike a gamete, a totipotent cell, a cell that has the potentiality to generate, by internal division and differentiation, all human types of cells. Indeed, given the profound, substantial change that happens at fertilization, "zygote" or "embryo" is a more accurate description than "fertilized egg."

In sum, the human gametes simply do not have the same potentiality that a zygote has. Two random gametes of the opposite type have the potentiality to fuse with each other, to lose their identity, and thus to give rise to a drastically new biological entity. But only the latter entity has the potentiality to further develop without loss of identity. It is thus from the zygote stage onward that respect is due. From that point, all the early human being needs to reach the adult stage is a supportive environment.

Twinning

Some object that—even if it is granted that the change from gametes to zygote marks a substantial change in biological identity—there is, from the zygote stage until fourteen or sixteen days after fertilization, a lack of identity with the adult organism (Smith and Brogaard 2003). The reasoning goes like this: an adult is an individual, but no embryo is a single individual because in its early stages it can divide and give rise to twins. It is potentially two (or more) individuals. The alleged conclusion to be drawn is that identity (the relation expressed by the phrase "is the same as") cannot jump the gap that separates the early stages of embryonic development from an adult individual. An embryo, on this account, is only a predecessor of an adult and is not, therefore, entitled to the same degree of respect as an adult.

The argument from twinning also fails. First, twinning is a rare phenomenon, and monozygotic twinning (twins from one egg) even more so. It is only the latter that is relevant for the argument because if the twins develop from the fertilization of two different eggs (and are thus dizygotic) they both are individuals from the start. It is only if they arise from a single zygote that the potentiality of an embryo to become more than one individual has to be assumed. However, the inference from the potentiality of a thing to be more than one to the conclusion that it is not actually one is a well-known logical fallacy. A stick in your hand is potentially two sticks: you can break it into two. But right now it is one stick. A flatworm wriggling its way along your desk is potentially two living flatworms: you could cut it with a knife. But right now it is one flatworm. Potential plurality is not inconsistent with actual unity. Therefore, it would be unwarranted to claim that the hundreds of thousands of human embryos that perhaps could have divided into two surviving embryos, but never did, were not individuals all along.

It is, moreover, sometimes claimed that an embryo lacks individuality because it is "only a cluster of cells," devoid of unified coordination (an argument along these lines is developed in DeGrazia 2006). This, however, is inconsistent with the empirical evidence. In July 2002 the scientific journal *Nature* published a report of several experiments with early mouse embryos (Pearson 2002). In one experiment a researcher painted the first two cells after the division of the zygote and tracked them down to a later (blastocyst) stage. It turned out that for the most part the inner mass cells came from one cell and the outer layer (trophectoderm) and other supporting tissues came from the other. The researcher concluded that the first division determines the fate of each cell and ultimately of all the tissues of the body. If, by analogy, this applies to humans, it shows that there is hardly a stage at which an embryo is merely a clump of disconnected cells. The unity that characterizes a complete organism, and therefore individuality, are present right from the start (Gómez-Lobo 2007; 2004b).

If each of the cells in an embryo begins to differentiate early on and thus ceases to be totipotent—that is, capable of generating an embryo by itself—how, then, can twinning be explained? Cloning or somatic cell nuclear transfer (SCNT) has brought to the fore a biological concept that may be of assistance in this context. When cloning works, the nucleus of a somatic cell that has long ago differentiated into a specific type of cell, like a skin cell, undergoes "reprogramming" so that the new cell into which that nucleus is inserted becomes dedifferentiated and capable of generating a new organism (Jaenisch 2004).[1] In the case of twinning, the nucleus of a cell within the early embryo (at the morula or blastocyst stage) is programmed for that cell to be a part of a whole, but if, say, a cell (a blastomere) produced during cleavage of the embryo emerges from the outer layer of the embryo (the zona pellucida), it can become reprogrammed back to a stage it had already left behind and thus give rise to a twin. This in turn explains why in mammals it is relatively easy to generate twins from a two-cell or a four-cell embryo, and why it becomes gradually more difficult in the case of more developed embryos. As differentiation progresses, reprogramming under natural conditions becomes more and more difficult until it disappears completely.

In human twinning there are two basic possibilities. In the case of twinning by budding, a blastomere separates off from an existing embryo to form a second embryo. (After birth, determining which one was the original embryo may be difficult or even impossible.) In the case of twinning by fission or division, more or less down the middle of an embryo, each born twin is identical to one of the two embryos that resulted from the division. The original embryo, although unified and in principle capable of continuing to develop, ceased to exist when it split into two. Its remains have been incorporated into—have become—the two twins because the reprogramming has changed the nature of the original cells (Damschen, Gómez-Lobo, and Schönecker 2006). Some critics reject this interpretation of twinning by fission as giving rise to two new embryos on the ground that mourning would be due for the embryo that disappeared when it divided, and mourning for such a lost embryo would be absurd. However, their argument is misguided. Mourning is an attitude one assumes at the death of someone one has known. Do we mourn the millions of people who die in Africa each year from malaria or malnutrition? Generally, we do not mourn the passing of people we do not know, even though they are undoubtedly people. In natural twinning, not even the mother has known, in any meaningful sense, the embryo from which the twins arise. In any event, the issue of the appropriateness of mourning is derivative and can be properly examined only after the nature of the early embryo has been settled on independent grounds. On such grounds, as we have seen, an embryo appears to be a unified human individual either from conception or, in the case of a twin, from the moment of reprogramming of the genome at budding or fission, and it remains the same individual into adulthood.

The ethical conclusion to be drawn is that, under the agreement that prohibits the intentional killing of adult persons, it would be wrong to destroy them when they were at the embryonic stage, or at any other stage, of their lives. Not to accept this is to engage in a gross form of discrimination on the basis of age. This also explains why the assignment of different degrees of "moral status" or "moral standing" to human beings should be rejected. To claim that an adult has "full moral status" but that an embryo has "lower status" or "an intermediate status" (between persons and things) is to assign to the same individual different values at different points of his or her life. This is intolerable in terms of moral protection from destructive action. That protection is meaningful only if it remains constant, if it is the same at every age. We should therefore uphold the traditional notion of equal dignity and equal protection of the very young, the mature, and the very old as a foundational principle of bioethics (Gómez-Lobo 2008).

Of course, if consequences alone determined the morality of an action, then the expected good results of embryo experimentation could be invoked to justify embryo destruction. (It is worth noting, however, that the remarkable advances that have been made in recent years developing medical treatments for conditions such as multiple sclerosis have been made using stem cells taken from adult, not embryonic, human beings [Prentice and Macrito 2013]. Moreover, a consequentialist should also take into account the happiness that the embryonic human beings and their parents—natural or adoptive—would enjoy if they were implanted and born, rather than destroyed by research.) But consequences alone do not determine the morality of an action. It is always wrong to intentionally kill (or enslave, or torture, or rape) one human being for the benefit of others. And the human embryo is a human being even though he or she is not yet mature enough to exercise reason and free choice. We human beings are basically bodies that are biologically programmed for the gradual development of the organs that support our mind. Our higher functions were radically present when we were in our embryonic stage of development. All human beings, even tiny embryos, share the same radical capacity for rationality, free will, and moral agency, a capacity that will—given a suitable environment and barring eventualities like accident or untimely death—in due course exhibit itself as an exercisable ability. We existed from our beginning, and our beginning was at our conception.

The conclusion must be that the intentional destruction of humans at the embryonic stage either for research or for other purposes is wrong because it is a violation of the principle of nonmaleficence, a violation that cannot be mitigated by predicted beneficial consequences. In the action itself, young human beings are intentionally harmed—indeed, destroyed. They are being deliberately deprived of the basic human good of life and of the prospect of a fully realized, flourishing life.

Note

1. See also the President's Council on Bioethics (2002, chap. 4).

Part II
ISSUES

Chapter 6

BEGINNING-OF-LIFE ISSUES

The choice of experimentation on human embryos as an example to lead us into the domain of bioethical thinking has already brought us into the field of moral problems concerning the beginning of peoples' lives. The main strategy in the previous chapter was to articulate and defend the common sense realization that we are basically bodily beings who grow and develop from our humble beginnings and without becoming something (or someone) else. As the permanence of our genome illuminates, we retain our identity through time in spite of many changes of appearance and performance. This identity thesis in turn paved the way for the following ethical argument:

(a)   If we should respect B, and

(b)   if A = B, then

(c)   we should respect A.

The proposed substitutions were "a human adult" for "B" and "a human embryo" for "A." The previous chapter relied on general agreement about (a) as an application of the principle of nonmaleficence. It was assumed that we all agree that it would be wrong to intentionally cause the death of an innocent adult. Only on the basis of such an agreement can the philosophical dialogue go forward. If someone thinks that it would be morally permissible to intentionally destroy human adults like you and me, then their view is so extreme that they place themselves outside the bounds of widely accepted bioethical norms and discourse. Thus, the previous chapter focused on showing that premise (b) is true. The chapter responded to three strategies that sought to show that premise (b) is false: the dualist view of human personhood, the reduction of potentiality to probability, and the invocation of twinning. Insofar as we have discredited these strategies and buttressed the common sense view, we have laid the groundwork for treating the rest of the moral issues that surround the early stages of life. Actions affecting very young human beings should be morally judged as we would judge actions affecting adults, that is, primarily in accordance with the principles of nonmaleficence and of beneficence. In the case of actions affecting competent adults, naturally enough, the principle of respect for their autonomy will also play an important role. Let us now examine a few highly controversial types of action that affect very young human beings.

Preimplantation Genetic Diagnosis

Preimplantation genetic diagnosis (PGD) is a relatively recently developed technique consisting of the extraction of one or two cells from a three-day embryo generated in vitro in order to identify certain genetic defects it may have. It is generally assumed that an embryo, that by then may comprise eight to sixteen cells, is not harmed by this early form of biopsy because of the compensation mechanism inherent in the embryo. It is thought that the expected role of the extracted cells will be played by other cells in accordance with the overall developmental pro gram of the organism. The aim of PGD is to decide whether to implant or not to implant a particular embryo in light of the results obtained. If the embryo appears to be abnormal or the carrier of an undesired trait, then he or she can be discarded. If not, then implantation in the woman's uterus may proceed. How should this practice be judged from a moral point of view?

The most common justification of PGD is utilitarian. The avoidance of the birth of a child affected with a genetic illness will spare the parents the unhappiness of raising and caring for such a child, while the birth of a normal child will lead them to experience happiness. The future avoidance of suffering and the promise of pleasure thus provide a clear-cut justification for PGD. An argument based on the autonomy of the parents can also be enlisted to buttress the utilitarian argument. Their free decision to reject the kind of child they do not want to have, and to have the kind of child they do want to have, would be, it could be claimed, an adequate reason to judge PGD morally acceptable. On this view, the choice of the parents, or of the mother alone (where the sperm was donated or purchased), if reached under conditions of full autonomy, would be ethical. There is an even more stringent argument that focuses on the consequences not for the parents but for the offspring. According to this view, "non-maleficence requires that we not harm people by causing them to experience significant pain and suffering over the balance of their lives" (Glannon 2005, 101). All three arguments are, however, unpersuasive. Let us first break down the practice of PGD into its component parts in order to examine them separately in light of the moral principles and the ontological claims defended in the foregoing chapters.

If we leave aside the action of in vitro fertilization as well as the standard generation of a plurality of embryos (neither of which is free from ethical objections[1]), the first action to consider is the extraction of the cell or cells for PGD. It is a general principle of medical ethics that interventions, especially interventions for which there is no consent on the part of the patient, can be justified if and only if they are performed for the good of the patient. This is a clear demand of the principle of beneficence. In this case the embryo, even if it were not exposed to significant risk from the procedure, clearly receives no benefit from it. In fact, it may be seriously deleterious to a human embryo to undergo PGD because the next action that may follow is that he or she is discarded. To discard or throw away an embryonic human being is to fail to provide the conditions for him or her to continue to live and is thus a violation of beneficence: the basic good of life of that human being has not been adequately sustained. Moreover, to discard an embryo because it is defective amounts to what might be called "negative eugenics," that is, the elimination of the disabled, the weak, and the unwanted. (This may be contrasted with "positive eugenics," which involves creating embryos with desired traits such as intelligence or strength.) Since the grounds for not wanting a child may range from serious genetic conditions, such as cystic fibrosis and Down syndrome, to not being of the desired sex or not having the desired eye color, there is no principled way of drawing a line once the practice of negative eugenics is accepted. By the end of the day, virtually *any* embryo could find himself or herself on this slippery slope, judged "undesirable" and eliminated.

The argument from autonomy, as we saw, does not have a problem with this particular version of the slippery slope, from serious genetic conditions to eye color, because it links the morality of an action to the free choice of the agent instead of the condition of the patient. But this cannot be right. As we saw earlier, the principle of autonomy, rightly understood, demands that free choices be respected provided there is no harm to others. As our analysis has shown, the discarded embryos do suffer harm: they are intentionally deprived of the conditions necessary to sustain the basic good of life.

The objection that young humans do not really suffer harm because they lack awareness is unpersuasive because, as we saw in our earlier discussion of nonmaleficence in chapter 2, there are many instances of being harmed without awareness of harm. If B steals books from his uncle's library, or traduces a colleague behind her back, B harms them both, even if they never find out what B has done. A correct analysis of harm, as we saw, should first and foremost identify the good or goods of which the victim is being deprived, regardless of her lack of awareness of the deprivation.

Moreover, the utilitarian argument for PGD based on consequences for the parents is objectionable because it violates human dignity at a deeper level. The idea of dignity, as we saw, entails the moral obligation to treat others as ends in themselves and not as mere means to our ends. If what justifies PGD is the future happiness of the parents, then children are clearly being viewed as mere instruments to their parents' happiness.

Someone could reply that compassion is also involved: PGD is intended to benefit not only the parents but also the child. The procedure allows a genetically defective child to be spared much suffering by being eliminated early on, which is precisely the point of the third argument. But this argument is paradoxical on two counts. It prescribes the destruction of certain embryos in the name of nonmaleficence—which is contradictory because destruction is a great harm—and it assumes that the cause of pain and suffering is not the genetic disorder but the refusal to destroy those affected by the disorder, which misplaces the causal explanation. It rests on a principle that has untoward implications when generalized: it justifies the elimination of suffering not by the alleviation of the condition itself but by elimination of those who suffer the condition. It would justify the idea of eliminating illnesses, such as HIV or sickle-cell anemia, by eliminating all those born with them. According to the principle of nonmaleficence, this is morally unacceptable.

We might also pause to ask what the eugenic elimination of those with serious genetic conditions says about, and to, those living with such conditions. Does not the practice of PGD and its endorsement by society send out the clear message that it is better not to be born than to be born with serious genetic conditions? We might also ask how many people with serious genetic conditions who have escaped the "quality control" filter of PGD agree with that judgment and wish they had never seen the light of day. Does PGD not constitute unjust discrimination against those with disabilities? If not, why not?

There is a further use of PGD that we have not considered. We have discussed the fear of genetic disease and the elimination of genetically defective embryos. But it is logically possible to choose not only against certain embryos but also in favor of some because they could be used to benefit others. One such possibility is the creation and selection of an embryo for implantation because its genome makes it a good source of cells, after birth, for transplantation to an ailing sibling. The justification for this would necessarily be consequentialist: the good consequences for the ailing brother or sister. But if we consider the action itself, not just its consequences, numerous concerns arise. The choice of a matching embryo spells the intentional destruction of the non-matching embryos, a destruction violating the principle of maleficence. Moreover, is not the production of a child as an instrument to benefit a sibling a violation of the basic dignity of a human being? Even if that child is loved and cared for afterward like any other, it remains true that the initial motivation for the generation of this particular human being was a goal beyond him or herself. Is not creating a child for the sake of another child akin to manufacturing a tool?

Is there a morally legitimate way of applying our newly gained genetic knowledge to alleviate suffering? If it is wrong to destroy a human being because he is the carrier of a mutation that may cause a serious disease, should we simply stand by and do nothing? No. If someone has reason to believe that she is the carrier of a mutated gene (because, say, of family history), then genetic testing is advisable. If it is established that she has a mutation that will lead, for example, to a monogenic disease (caused, that is, by a mutation in one copy of a gene, such as Huntington's disease), then she could ethically decide to abstain from procreation. There is a huge moral difference between, on the one hand, not conceiving a child and, on the other, eliminating a child at the early stages of his or her life. In the latter case a human being is intentionally harmed; in the former case no one is harmed.

A further legitimate application of genetic knowledge is the attempt to correct the genetic defect in the cells that may cause a disease. Somatic cell gene therapy has as its goal the core aim of medicine, restoring the condition of the patient to normal standards of health and well-functioning, not the elimination of the patient. This form of therapy is still at an early stage (Knapton 2015) and is not without risks. An even more distant prospect is a treatment called germ-line genetic therapy. The distinct feature of this approach is to correct a genetic defect in the gametes of adults in order to prevent the mutation from being passed along to their children and thus to future generations. However, we presently do not know what side effects the apparently beneficial manipulation of the genome might bring about. Moreover, if the genetic mutation to be corrected also happens to confer benefits in a certain environment, such as higher resistance to malaria in the case of those afflicted by sickle-cell anemia in Africa, then we might be harming future generations who will have to live in that environment without that resistance.

Aside from the risk of harming individuals or future generations, both forms of gene therapy are guided by the principle of beneficence and do not involve maleficence (as understood here, that is, there is no intention to eliminate or harm anyone). Both are morally acceptable projects (if engaged in with proper risk assessment) and ought to be researched.

Abortion

If, as we have seen, there are sound reasons for rejecting both destructive embryo research and the elimination of "defective" embryos, it seems reasonable also to reject the intentional killing of human beings beyond the embryonic stage. The arguments that are used to justify embryo research and embryo selection—the advancement of biomedical knowledge and the prevention of suffering from genetic disease—are difficult to apply to abortion. Abortion does nothing to advance our knowledge of fetal development, and the vast majority of fetuses who are aborted are perfectly normal. If the standard consequentialist arguments employed to justify embryo destruction have little application to the issue of abortion, what might?[2]

Let us recall the basic facts surrounding abortion. We mentioned in the previous chapter that Edwards and Steptoe, the IVF pioneers, describe the early human embryo as a "microscopic human being" (1981, 83). As standard biology textbooks teach, a human embryo with its full complement of human chromosomes comes into being at fertilization. For example, one textbook reads: "Human development begins at fertilization when a sperm fuses with an oocyte [egg] to form a single cell—a zygote. This highly specialized, totipotent cell marks the beginning of each of us as a unique individual" (Moore, Persaud, and Torchia 2011, 13).[3] Another reads: "The development of a human being begins with fertilization" (Sadler 1990, 1). Once he or she has been implanted in the uterus and the possibility of spontaneous twinning has ended, the unified development of the new organism can be closely followed by modern methods of observation such as sonograms. There can be no doubt that an integrated, self-directed organism is growing through well-known stages and that (if all goes well) a child will be born, who will one day be able to read these pages, just like you.

Is it apt, it might be asked, to refer to the fetus as a "child"? We speak of a child after birth, but it is perfectly natural to speak also of a child before birth. Indeed, the first definition of "child" given in the *Oxford English Dictionary* is "The unborn or newly born human being; foetus, infant."[4] And it is standard, outside the abortion context, for people to use the words "child" and "baby," rather than "fetus," in relation to the unborn. For example, we naturally say that a woman has "conceived a child," and we ask a pregnant woman "How is the baby doing?" not "How is the fetus doing?"[5] Government health departments issue publications explaining how an unborn "baby" grows and advising women against conduct that may harm their unborn baby. For example, *The Pregnancy Book*, published by the UK Department of Health, describes "how your baby develops from the day you conceive until you give birth" (UK Department of Health 2009, 18). It explains (quoting the medical terminology of "embryo" and "fetus" to describe different stages of development): "In the very early weeks, the developing baby is called an embryo. From about eight weeks, it is called a fetus" (18). The book advises against the consumption of certain types of food or drink that may harm the baby: "There are some foods that you should not eat when you are pregnant because they may make you ill or harm your baby" (26). (Note the perfectly natural use of the word "harm" in relation to the child, even though the child may be completely unaware of being harmed.) It cautions: "Every cigarette you smoke harms your baby. Cigarettes restrict the essential oxygen supply to your baby. So their tiny heart has to beat harder every time you smoke"(30). Historically a pregnant woman was described, in common parlance and in the law, as "with child."[6] And the preamble to the UN Declaration on the Rights of the Child notes that "the child, by reason of his physical and mental immaturity, needs special safeguards and care, including appropriate legal protection, before as well as after birth" (United Nations 1959). In the context of the abortion debate, is it not use of the word "fetus" rather than "child" that should raise questions? Does the use of "fetus" rather than the more natural and usual terms "child" and "baby" not serve (deliberately or otherwise) to dehumanize and depersonalize the unborn (see Finnis 2010)? To avoid any such danger, "human fetus" and "unborn child" will both be used hereafter to mean the same: the human being from conception to delivery.

Only determined dualists could evade the conclusion that the organism developing in his or her mother's womb deserves respect. If dualists conclude that the unborn child does not deserve respect, they have to face the challenge of pinpointing the occurrence of the substantial change that makes a child before birth and an adult drastically different sorts of beings. In the view of someone who adopted a consistent dualist approach, it would have to be an extrabiological event. If the reply, however, is that the mind begins to "occupy" the body when the brain is activated and sentience becomes possible, it faces the problem that even the "arrival" of the mind was already determined from the very start by the zygote's genetic constitution, that this "arrival" is merely one stage in gradual self-directed development, and that it does not represent a radical new departure. The beginning of sentience is a programmed step and does not mark a substantial change. Accordingly, the "moral status" of an adult and of a very young human being must be the same. As we have argued, they are the same sort of being, simply at different stages of development.

When you were an embryo at your conception, or your implantation in the womb, or when your organs began to form, or when you attained the ability to survive outside the womb, or when you were born, or when you started school, or when you went to college, was it not *you* all along, albeit growing, developing, unfolding in line with your remarkable and self-directed genetic endowment? If your mother opened the family photo album, pointed to an ultrasound photograph taken when she was pregnant, and said: "This was you at six months after conception," would you reply "No, mum, you're mistaken. That's not me. That's just a biological organism. *I* didn't begin to exist until I was about four years old, when I became self-conscious, when my mind began to inhabit that biological organism"?

However, abortion, by its very nature, generates a set of problems that do not arise in the case of research on in vitro embryos, where the key issue is the ontological status of early human beings. Abortion presupposes a pregnancy, and a pregnancy involves two individuals: the mother and the child. The objection that an unborn child is just a "part" of the maternal organism, like an arm or a leg, is factually wrong, not least because of the genetic difference between the two. Moreover, the every move of an obstetrician during prenatal care is grounded on the assumption of the distinctness of the child developing in his or her mother's womb. No one is surprised by the realization that after the delivery the child has a perfectly independent biological trajectory from the mother, a trajectory that started at conception.

Some defenders of abortion concede that abortion ends the life of a human being. For example, Peter Singer, a leading utilitarian bioethicist, has written: "It is possible to give 'human being' a precise meaning. We can use it as equivalent to 'member of the species *Homo sapiens*'. Whether a being is a member of a given species is something that can be determined scientifically by an examination of the nature of the chromosomes in the cells of living organisms. In this sense there is no doubt that from the first moments of its existence, an embryo conceived from human sperm and eggs [*sic*] is a human being" (Singer 2011, 73).[7] Some bioethicists nevertheless justify abortion on the ground that, although the unborn child is a human being, it has no right to life because it lacks mental abilities like self-awareness. Other bioethicists justify abortion by claiming that any rights the child has can be outweighed by the rights of the mother. If a woman wants to have a child and acts accordingly, there is no conflict. But if a woman does not want to have a child and yet becomes pregnant, then, it is claimed, she has a "right" to terminate the pregnancy. This right may conflict with a "right" of the child to use her body, but, defenders of this view add, the right of the mother overrides the right of her child. Therefore, abortion is justified.

This is the basic pattern of an argument, which may be filled in by adding more detailed specifications. For example, one can claim that the "granting of the right" to the child to use the mother's body depends on the manner of initiation of the pregnancy. If it was fully voluntary on the part of the woman, the child has indeed been granted the right to be there. If the pregnancy was due, say, to contraceptive failure and hence was not fully voluntary, its right is compromised. If it was completely involuntary, due to rape, it has no right to be in her body.[8]

A further qualification that is sometimes added concerns the reasons the mother invokes to exercise her "right" to terminate the pregnancy. A late-term abortion for a trivial reason, such as not wanting to cancel a vacation, would not be justified, whereas an early abortion requested by a teen-age girl whose education would be jeopardized by continuation of the pregnancy would be justified. It should be noted that this type of argument seeks to show that even if the humanity or personhood of the fetal human being is acknowledged, it does not follow that abortion is wrong. Since the identity thesis summarized at the beginning of this chapter acknowledges the humanity of an unborn child, it follows that the "conflict of rights" approach, if correct, would represent a more serious challenge to the case against abortion than the strategy of denying that very young human beings have rights.

How should we evaluate the alleged conflict of rights? The notion of rights has been the subject of intense philosophical discussion at least since the seventeenth century, and it is impossible to do justice to it in the present context. For our purposes it suffices to sketch a sense of the term "right" that roughly matches its use in the ethical debate on abortion. That use is not uniform, and it covers both negative and positive rights. No attempt is made to assess the legal framework of abortion rights (if any) within a specific country or legal system, although for the sake of clarity some of the illustrations used will involve legal rights.

First, it seems that to have a moral right is to have either a justified claim against being interfered with in one's enjoyment of something or a positive claim to something. Just wanting or desiring something does not create a right. Peter may want to own his neighbor's car, but that does not make Peter the owner. His purchase of the car gives him title to it. On the other hand, not wanting or not desiring something does not nullify a right.[9] Alexandra may not desire to own some property bequeathed to her, but she is the rightful owner until she disposes of it. Second, a moral right, either positive or negative, does not require consciousness or awareness of the right or its object. After the death of her uncle in Texas, Georgiana may have acquired property rights to his estate, but she may not know it because her cousins are withholding the contents of her uncle's will. Likewise, a permanently unconscious person can have property rights of which she is totally unaware. Third, a right has to be a claim to protection in or possession of something acknowledged to be good. It would be absurd to claim a right to be mugged or raped.

With the foregoing in mind we may now turn to the moral justification of abortion in those cases in which there is said to be a conflict of rights between mother and child. When would the rights of the mother override those of the child? A dualist might reply that they always override because the rights of an actual person defeat those of a potential person (Warren 1973, 7). But we have already shown that this formulation is inadequate because having the potentiality for the exercise of higher human faculties (which is what the term "potential person" alludes to) does not exclude the actuality of being a human person. The potentiality for the exercise of those higher faculties is nothing other than an actual radical capacity inherent, now, in the unborn child. The ability to exercise that capacity must await the child's maturing, but an ability must not be confused with a capacity. A human being can have a capacity for higher mental abilities without (yet) being able to exercise those abilities, just as you now have the capacity to speak Russian but may not (yet) have the ability to do so.

Since the mother and the child are on the same footing with regard to being human, the key consideration will be the specific rights that are pitted against each other, and these in turn will depend on the goods at stake, since rights are specified by the goods they seek to secure. Let us start with the unborn child. Given that an abortion is an action whose goal is the death of the child in order to interrupt the pregnancy it is clear that the good at stake is the good of life. Since the developing child is enjoying the good of life, it is fair to say that she has a justified claim not to be deprived of it, under the principle of nonmaleficence. This negative right does not depend on consciousness. The good of life sustains consciousness but can be possessed without it. People who are sleeping do not lose their right to life, nor do those in a coma, even if the coma is irreversible. It is still wrong to intentionally kill them.

Someone might object that abortion does not involve an intention to kill the unborn child, that it amounts merely to intentionally detaching the child from the mother and that, if it were possible to nurture the child in an artificial womb—which has, unfortunately, yet to be invented—that should be done. This is an objection that must be taken seriously because it embodies the deeper attitude of disengagement that underlies the alleged conflict of rights. However, the description of standard abortion procedures as merely "detaching" a fetus is inaccurate. It would be disingenuous to claim that an action that marshals means (whether chemical or surgical) to ensure the death of a fetus is not performed with the intention of securing its death. This is precisely what abortionists seek to achieve: a dead baby. This is their aim even when the baby is viable and perfectly capable of surviving if only allowed to emerge alive.[10] In contrast to abortion, a cesarean section performed after viability to allow a child to continue to live outside the mother's body satisfies the description of "detachment," and from what it involves (carefully cutting through the woman's abdomen without touching the baby, having an incubator and neonatologist at the ready, etc.), it is clear that it is an action of a drastically different nature from abortion.

In order to assess the merits of the conflict argument conclusively, we have to turn to the rights of the mother. Which are the goods that ground her rights and of which she would be deprived if the pregnancy continued? The good most commonly mentioned in this context is a woman's control over her own body (though, of course, abortion standardly involves interference with the body of another: the unborn child). The point is often conveyed by enumerating evils (i.e., bad things or nonmoral "bads") that would follow upon the continuation of the pregnancy: the burden of motherhood at a young age; risk to health; the stigma of being an unwed mother (although this is less important today than it used to be); the prospect of raising a child alone because the father has disappeared; the additional financial, physical, and emotional stress for a woman who already has children; the loss of career opportunities; the limitations and inconveniences imposed by the pregnancy, and so on. Since it is rational to avoid evils, it would seem that there is a right to avoid them, and that this would be the paramount right.

It is possible, however, to take a more radical stand and hold that the central right is simply "the right to choose," a negative right that protects and secures the good of autonomy itself. The goods and evils of the pregnancy and its aftermath do not really matter. What matters on this view are the desires of the mother and what she chooses to do, regardless of what she in fact chooses, as long as her choice is autonomous. In popular language this is often stressed by saying that "a woman should not be forced to go through an unwanted pregnancy" and "it is her choice and her choice alone." Is the appeal to radical autonomy, that is, to the right to satisfy any desire regardless of its object, a rational appeal? Surely not. It is obvious that we sometimes desire things that are good and sometimes things that are bad. We have right and wrong desires.[11] Autonomy by itself does not guarantee morally right action. Freely choosing to have an abortion does not tell us whether the choice was right or wrong any more than freely choosing to kill one's child after birth tells us whether that choice was right or wrong. To judge the morality of abortion, we have to consider the human goods or, more narrowly, we should consider whether the principle of nonmaleficence is being violated, for, as we saw earlier, possible and actual violations of nonmaleficence impose strict limitations on autonomy. If an autonomous action causes significant harm to someone, then it should not be performed.

It is clear that abortion negatively affects the life of the child: he or she is deprived of the human good that sustains the enjoyment of all other goods. The goods of which the mother is deprived if the pregnancy continues do not seem to be comparable to the loss of life. Although the pregnancy may be extremely hard to bear, she continues to live. The burdens of pregnancy can be severe and have lasting effects. But they can also be relatively minor and transient. Many women maintain a fairly normal routine of life and work well into pregnancy. (Occasionally a woman gives birth without even knowing that she has been pregnant.[12]) Further, we standardly expect fathers to bear significant burdens in relation to children they have fathered even if they had no intention of having a child and did everything they could to prevent conception. Many fathers are ordered by courts to pay tens of thousands of dollars to provide for their children, however unwanted, until the child reaches the age of majority, on pain of imprisonment. And this is simply because they are biologically the child's father.

Moreover, if after the baby is born the mother gives the baby up for adoption, the mother may be restored to external conditions similar to those she enjoyed previously in terms of opportunity and freedom. Granted, her emotional condition may never be the same as before going through the burdensome process of carrying and nurturing her unborn child and then giving the child away after birth. But there may well be burdens—physical, mental, and emotional—involved in having an abortion; the burdens are by no means necessarily only one way. Again, if the mother changes her mind about having an abortion and welcomes the child, she may find herself enjoying a new set of human goods, such as the goods of maternity and love, goods subsumed under the Aristotelian concept of friendship.

None of this is meant to trivialize the difficult, sometimes agonizing predicament of an unwanted pregnancy, but it does represent an effort to bring rational clarity to bear on a difficult choice. If real goods are protected and one is not deflected by apparent evils, the result will be rational and morally right choice, however difficult.

One argument worth mentioning starts with dualist assumptions but reaches a countercultural conclusion, namely, that abortion is indeed wrong. This is the "Future Like Ours" argument developed by Don Marquis. The argument starts from the allegedly unproblematic assumption that it is seriously wrong to kill an adult because "the loss of one's life deprives one of all the experiences, activities, projects, and enjoyments that would otherwise have constituted one's future" (Marquis 1989). The argument runs that abortion produces the same loss of a future in the case of a fetus and, therefore, the killing of a human fetus is seriously wrong. The key feature of this argument is that, unlike most anti-abortion arguments, it does not focus on the goodness of life but on the goodness of future conscious experiences. And the goodness consists basically in those future experiences being pleasant. However, the main difficulty of making future consciousness and the expectation of pleasant mental experiences the cornerstone of respect is that it weakens the moral protection of the old, the suffering, and the mentally handicapped. The older you are and the less of a pleasant future you have, the less you deserve protection. If you are old, ill, mentally confused, and in pain, what protection, if any, do you have? Marquis holds: "If the patient's future is intolerable, whatever his or her immediate past, we want our account to allow killing the patient" (Marquis 1989, 197). This remark, with its perplexing admission of a specific intention in setting up the argument, could reasonably be regarded as a *reductio ad absurdum* of the argument itself. If an assumption about the human good to be protected leads to a radical rejection of equal protection of human beings (which is a violation of justice), then the assumption should be dropped. Assuming that life is the key good docs not lead to such non-egalitarian consequences because there is no reason to assign different values to different lives in accordance with the outstanding amount of time that they have left or the amount of future pleasurable experiences they are expected to have.

In short, then, abortion is a type of action that violates the principle of nonmaleficence because it intentionally destroys the life of an already existing human being, and there are no countervailing goods to be preserved and promoted that could justify it. But is the removal of the unborn child justifiable if the intention is not to kill the child but to save the life of the mother? Let us consider an important principle of natural law ethics that can justify the removal of the unborn child in rare cases where is it not intended, but merely foreseen, that the child will die as a result: the "principle of double effect."[13]

Double-Effect Reasoning

The principle of double effect (PDE) is a sophisticated conceptual tool that provides a criterion to discern when an action that negatively affects an instance of a human good is not really a violation of nonmaleficence. It was developed under several assumptions. One is the anticonsequentialist thesis that it is not only results or consequences that matter but also the action itself, and that the action itself is determined in turn by the proximate intention of the agent. A further assumption is that there is an objective set of human goods, of which human life is one. The idea that someone might benefit from death is regarded as irrational because the ending of pain and suffering would be achieved by eliminating the person herself. She would no longer be there to reap any benefit.[14]

In its standard formulation the PDE reads:

An action that has a good and a bad effect is morally permissible if and only if the following conditions are satisfied:

(1) The action itself is not morally incorrect—that is, does not violate by itself any moral norm and ultimately the principles of beneficence and nonmaleficence;

(2) The good effect intended by the agent is not achieved through the bad effect;

(3) The bad effect is not intended by the agent but only foreseen and tolerated; and

(4) There is proportionality between the good effect and the bad one. If the good effect is minimal and the bad effect considerable, such that there is no proportionality, the action will be wrong. Moreover, if there is an alternative course of action that does not involve producing the bad effect, that course should be followed.

The literature on the PDE, both supportive and critical, is voluminous.[15] This is not the place to provide a thorough justification of its traditional and common use in medical ethics (and other contexts[16]). One objection deserves to be mentioned because of its broader implications. It has been doubted that the difference between intending a bad effect and merely foreseeing it is morally significant. One reason given is that one can intend two or more outcomes—one good, one bad—by performing a single action (Glannon 2005, 126–27). This is of course true, but it is not a genuine objection to the PDE. The principle is normative, and it states that if indeed an agent aims both at the good *and* the bad effect, the action will be morally wrong because condition (3) has not been met. Another objection is that we can never know what an agent's intention is or was. But this is to confuse two things: on the one hand, the conceptual and real distinction between intention and foresight, and on the other, the feasibility of ascertaining or proving intention in a given case. In any event, as the operation of criminal justice systems around the world shows, juries are perfectly capable of deciding in many cases (on the basis of evidence such as admissions by the accused, testimony by witnesses, and relevant circumstances) whether a defendant intended a consequence, foresaw a consequence, or did neither.

Real life, with its pervasive intertwining of goods and evils, requires us to appeal to the PDE lest we remain paralyzed when confronted with the likelihood or certainty of the bad effects of our actions. Many good courses of action have likely or inevitable bad side effects, but this is hardly an argument for abstaining from good actions and remaining frozen in the face of life. Applying the PDE is not always easy, and its various applications can sometimes look like contrived and hair-splitting forms of reasoning. But in many cases its application is clear. Moreover, the PDE has long been accepted by professional medical ethics. Further, it is also at the heart of the criminal law in countries like the

United States and England. Last but not least, the key distinction at the heart of the principle, between intended and foreseen consequences, accords with common sense. (Even a dog, it has been said, knows the difference between being tripped over and being kicked.) Let us consider just a few examples.

A dentist foresees that the extraction of four wisdom teeth will cause her patient considerable discomfort. A teacher foresees that when he teaches calculus, some student or other in the class is going to get the wrong end of the stick and misunderstand the truth he is trying to convey. A doctor who administers chemotherapy to a little girl to cure her cancer foresees that, as an unavoidable side effect of the therapy, her hair will fall out and she will feel nauseous. To cite an actual historical example, in the Second World War, Gen. Dwight Eisenhower foresaw, when he ordered the allied troops to liberate France, that thousands of allied soldiers would be killed by the Germans. These are all bad side effects of good actions, actions that are ethical because the bad side effects are merely foreseen, are not the means to the good effects, and are in proportion to the good effects. The actions would, by contrast, be quite different and bad if the dentist intended her patient to suffer discomfort, if the teacher intended the student to misunderstand calculus, if the doctor intended the little girl to suffer hair loss and nausea, and if General Eisenhower intended his soldiers to be killed.

A standard hypothetical to illustrate the application of the PDE is in fact drawn from the beginning of life. Tiffany has been diagnosed with a cancerous uterus. She is told by her physician, Dr. Michaels, that unless it is removed promptly she will die, but that if it is removed she will survive. He also informs her that tests have shown that she is four months pregnant and that the child will die if the uterus is removed. Tiffany is delighted to hear that the removal of her uterus will save her life, but very sad that her child will die as a result. May Dr. Michaels, with Tiffany's consent, remove her uterus in order to save her life, merely foreseeing the death of her child? According to natural law ethics, he may. Applying the PDE, Dr. Michaels would be acting ethically because (1) to remove a cancerous uterus is a morally permissible action; (2) saving Tiffany's life is not achieved through the bad effect of the child's death but by the removal of her cancerous uterus (Tiffany will survive irrespective of whether her child dies or, miraculously, survives); (3) Dr. Michaels does not intend the death of the child but only foresees it; and

(4) there is a proportionate reason for removing the child: the saving of Tiffany's life. In other words, if all the conditions spelled out by the PDE have been satisfied, the bad outcome, the incidental shortening of the child's life, is not in violation of nonmaleficence.

What if it is not a cancerous uterus but the pregnancy itself that is threatening the mother's life? If such cases exist in developed societies with modern medical facilities, they must be rare indeed. But let us assume that we are faced with a case in which, if the unborn child is not removed, the mother will die. This is a difficult question, and not all upholders of natural law ethics would agree on the answer. But a good case can be made that the PDE could apply to justify the removal of the child. Of course, every reasonable effort should be made to try to gestate the child to the point at which it would be viable and could therefore survive upon removal. If, however, this is not possible, and if without the removal of a nonviable child the mother will die, then a good case can be made that removal would be justified by the PDE. Given that the intention in removing the child would be to save the mother, and that the child's death would be a merely foreseen, regrettable side effect of this life-saving procedure, it would be misleading to describe the procedure as an "abortion" at all, for abortion involves an intention to kill the unborn child.

If the PDE can be used to remove an unborn child in order to save the mother's life, could it not also be used to justify removal where the mother's health is at risk, or where the pregnancy resulted from rape? No. The fourth requirement of the PDE requires there to be a proportionate reason for removal. Only life is proportionate to life. Nothing less than saving the mother's life is proportionate to an action that results in the death of her child (Gómez-Lobo 2002, 95–96).[17]

The alternative to adopting the PDE is giving up one of the rock-bottom principles of morality: nonmaleficence. If, however, you are willing to morally justify the intentional attack on a basic human good (as most bioethicists are), then you will have little time for the PDE.

Whether abortion is morally justifiable is a general question in bioethics. Whether doctors should perform abortions is a narrower question within the field of professional medical ethics. A satisfactory answer will have to appeal to principles and norms specific to the profession. One central assumption about physicians (which justifies the great social prestige they have enjoyed) is that they are healers, that is, that they are bound by a moral norm that bids them cure the sick. The pertinent question then is whether pregnancy is an illness and abortion a therapy. We shall return to the question about what constitutes a therapy in the next chapter when we examine physician-assisted suicide.

Infanticide

Most people would recoil at the thought of deliberately killing a newborn baby, especially if it were their own child, but such feelings could be perhaps neutralized by reminders of the apparently widespread practice of infanticide in many cultures. In fact, ethical discussions of infanticide usually begin with a review of anthropological data pointing to the custom of eliminating weak or deformed infants not only in primitive cultures but also among the highly civilized Greeks and Romans (Tooley 1983, 315–18; Engelhardt 1996, 228–29). In philosophical ethics, however, the extent of a practice, no matter how pervasive, carries little weight. As we noted in chapter 1, moral norms cannot be derived from anthropological observation. The observation that individuals a, b, c, d, e, and so on, usually perform actions of type T only tells us that many individuals (of a class, or a culture, or a time period, etc.) perform actions of type T, but it does not tell us whether actions of type T are morally right or not. Furthermore, the fact that people, say, from an ancient culture thought that certain classes of action were right still does not tell us whether they *are* right or not. It is a reasonably well-attested fact that certain actions and institutions, such as slavery, are believed at a certain time to be right and it subsequently becomes clear that they are not. The same can happen with types of action initially believed to be wrong and later regarded as permissible, such as the charging of interest on loans. In this sense, then, it is meaningful to speak about the history of moral thought. Moral beliefs about kinds of action have changed, but whether the change has been for good or ill, whether there has been progress or regress, is an independent question to be settled in light of considerations both ethical and ontological. Although infanticide of normal newborns seems to have been (and still is) practiced in different parts of the world, especially in order to eliminate girls (Bouillon-Jensen and Larson 2004), it is fair to say that most people have come to think that it is wrong to kill healthy babies. Reports about female infanticide or "gendercide" in India (to avoid the burden of providing dowries) and in China (to have a male child for support in old age, given that country's draconian "one child" policy) meet with widespread disapproval. The bioethical debate today generally (but not exclusively; see Giubilini and Minerva 2013, and response by Finnis 2013) concerns the killing of seriously disabled or terminally ill newborns.

In the case of disabled newborns the argument for their active elimination is utilitarian. It is anticipated that otherwise they and their families will lead lives of great suffering and that by eliminating the child at an early age the suffering of both the child and the family will be eliminated or at least attenuated. The difficulties confronting this form of reasoning also arise in respect of other utilitarian arguments. Assumptions are often made about the future condition of a person that may turn out to be false. Someone born with a disability may not experience intolerable suffering. Indeed, it seems to be the case generally that persons with even severe disabilities view their own condition much more favorably than those without those disabilities, and certainly do not wish to be killed or wish they had been killed in infancy.

Some infants are born with disabilities that are crippling but not life threatening. Others are expected to die shortly after birth: a prominent example is that of children born with anencephaly, a malformation of the head that usually results in the lack of large portions of the brain. Such a child will usually die shortly after birth and presumably does not experience pain, depending on the areas of the brain that are absent. Advocates of infanticide tend to focus on the prospect of removing high-quality organs for transplantation, if the organ retrieval team were allowed to remove them while the child is still alive. In support of the infanticide of such newborns, it is argued that, because they lack a complete brain, even if they survived they would never be able to exercise the higher human mental functions, such as thought and choice. These newborns are not, therefore, "persons" and never will be, and do not merit moral protection. One response to this line of argument would focus on the fact that these babies are human beings. They are undoubtedly seriously disabled and lack the organic basis to exercise many human abilities, but they are human beings nevertheless. They are therefore entitled to the same protection as other human beings. They may not be able to exercise higher mental functions, but neither can normal newborn babies, or adults in a permanent coma, some adults who have sustained serious brain injury in accidents at work or on the roads, or adults with advanced dementia. Moreover, with regard to taking organs from anencephalic newborns (even with parental consent) it stands to reason that, since their natural death can be anticipated with some degree of accuracy and measures can be taken for the oxygenation, preparation, and retrieval of their organs shortly after natural death, their organs would be only slightly less viable than if the organs were removed before death. The benefits to others of organ transplantation no more justify the killing of the disabled (or nondisabled) newborn than they justify the team of paramedics in our scenario involving Stan, when they left him to die (see chapter 3).

In sum, as embryo research and abortion inflict deadly harm on the early human being, depriving him or her of the good of life, they are unethical. This is so even though adult agents may autonomously wish to carry out embryo research or have an abortion.

Young human beings, like embryos and unborn children, lack autonomy. Let us now turn to issues that for the most part do involve autonomous choices, including the intentional ending of a patient's life at his or her request.

Notes

1. See Finnis (2011c, 298–300) for the natural law argument that IVF is ethically objectionable, even where a single embryo is created and then implanted, as bringing persons into being in a manner akin to the manufacture of products.

2. On the ethics of abortion, see also Gómez-Lobo (2002, chap. 7).

3. For a list of texts, see George and Tollefsen (2011, 266–68).

4. It continues: "When the application was subsequently extended, the primitive sense was often expressed by *babe, baby, infant*; but 'child' is still the proper term, and retained in phrases such as 'with child.'" *Oxford English Dictionary* 1989, vol. 3, 113; emphasis original.

5. The headnote to the English case of *Paton v. Trustees of BPAS* [1979] QB 276 begins: "A wife, who had conceived a child by her husband, was concerned about her pregnancy."

6. See, for example, in England, sections 58 and 59 of the Offences against the Person Act 1861. For the historical development of the law relating to abortion in England, see Keown (1988), and in the United States, see Dellapenna (2006).

7. See also his video-recorded debate on the moral status of the fetus with John Finnis and Margaret Little (Princeton 2010).

8. For Judith Thomson's famous argument that even if the unborn child is a person, it does not follow that the child has a right that the mother act like a

"Good Samaritan" by continuing the pregnancy, see Thomson (1971). For a response, see Kaczor (2015, 152–87).

9. For the opposite view, see Tooley (1983, 100–123).

10. Contrary to popular belief, the US Supreme Court in *Roe v. Wade* 410 US 113 (1973) upheld a right to abortion even after viability, if in the interests of the woman's health. And in the companion case of *Doe v. Bolton* 410 US 179, 192 (1973) "health" was broadly defined.

11. Aristotle, *Nicomachean Ethics* VI. 2. 1139a 21–31, http://dx.doi.org/10.4159 /DLCL.aristotle-nicomachean_ethics.1926.

12. For a recent example, see Davies (2014).

13. For the possible application of the principle to conduct resulting in the death of an unborn child, see also Gómez-Lobo (2002, 92–96).

14. The longing for death often expressed by Christian mystics should be understood as a desire to attain the subsequent good of the bodily resurrection, not the elimination of the self.

15. For supporters, see, for example, Cavanaugh (2006) and Finnis (2011a). For critics see, for example, Glover (1991, chap. 6) and Glannon (2005, 126–29).

16. Contexts such as war, where natural law ethics opposes the intentional killing of noncombatants but may permit acts that foreseeably result in their death as a side effect of proportionate military action. See, generally (as well as for an ethical critique of the possession of nuclear weapons), Finnis, Boyle, and Grisez (1988).

17. Occasionally an ethicist within the natural law tradition suggests that the removal of the child in other circumstances, such as rape, would also be proportionate, but this is a distinctly minority view.

Chapter 7

END-OF-LIFE ISSUES

The vantage point for judging the beginning-of-life issues discussed in the previous chapter was the goodness of life. Since to harm someone is to deprive them of a good, and since life, while not a supreme good, is the good that in a sense grounds all other goods, the conclusion was that under the principle of nonmaleficence the intentional killing of young human beings—embryo destruction, abortion, and infanticide—were all gravely unethical. This vantage point, however, can be and has been challenged. It is well known that there are people who believe that their lives are not good—indeed, that they would be "better off dead." It is typically this belief, whether held explicitly or implicitly, that motivates those who attempt to commit suicide, those who seek aid in committing suicide, and those who request euthanasia.[1]

How should we judge these three types of action? At first sight they seem to fall under different principles so that reflection and discernment are required to determine the appropriate vantage point from which to make a judgment. If these actions are classed as self-destructive, it seems that they must be subsumed under the prohibition of maleficence. However, two objections could be raised. First, the person herself claims to be acting in pursuit of a good, or at least in avoidance of an evil, as it appears to her. She claims that death would be a benefit, not a harm to her. The second objection is that the alleged harm is not inflicted upon someone else, so that the standard restriction of autonomy (to prevent harm to others) does not apply.

Since we are dealing here with different types of action and different forms of agency, it will be useful to classify the types according to the degree of medical intervention in the act itself. In the case of a person who commits suicide by, say, jumping from a bridge or in front of a train, the agent is the person herself and there is no medical agency involved. In physician-assisted suicide (PAS), a medical professional aids the person who commits suicide by providing the means for her to end her life, such as a prescription for a lethal dosage of drugs. In the case of euthanasia, the agency does not lie with the person herself but with the physician or health care professional who causes her death, typically by administering a lethal injection.

In all three cases the intention of the agent to cause death is essential. Accidentally slipping in front of a train is not suicide. Mistakenly handing a lethal dose of pills to a patient who later takes them is not PAS. Switching off a life-support machine because the patient finds it too burdensome is not euthanasia. Again, in the case of the captain who stays on the sinking ship to try to ensure that everyone else has been evacuated, and of the pilot who stays at the controls of his plane to steer it away from a densely populated area, death is neither intended nor self-inflicted. If, on the other hand, death is freely chosen and self-inflicted, as in the case of a Buddhist monk who sets himself on fire to protest against oppressive policies, it is suicide.

Thus, the fundamental question is whether it is ever morally right to intentionally cause one's death (suicide), or for a physician intentionally to help a patient to commit suicide (PAS), or to intentionally end the life of a patient at her request (voluntary euthanasia). Is the principle of nonmaleficence being violated or is the principle of beneficence being followed? The correct answer to this question depends on the validity of the claim that one's life, or the life of the person requesting to be killed, is indeed bad, that life is no longer "worth living." If a person would indeed be "better off dead," then by terminating their life, one is ridding them of an evil and thereby benefiting them. Many bioethicists today endorse PAS or euthanasia. For example, Beauchamp and Childress endorse PAS if certain conditions are satisfied, not least an autonomous request by the patient, and suffering unacceptable to the patient (Beauchamp and Childress 2013, 184–85).

The Alleged Badness of a Person's Life

If Sandra says her life is bad, how can one doubt that it is in fact bad for her? Isn't it presumptuous to pretend to know better than Sandra herself? This is an old and complex problem in philosophy (see Plato, *Theaetetus*, 151e–164b) that cannot be exhaustively explored here, where we are confining ourselves to the basics of bioethics. However, the following considerations should be helpful in thinking through these issues clearly.

It is common knowledge that we are not always right, that we make mistakes about what we take to be true, and that we are particularly prone to self-deception with regard to our own good. Anyone who has ever regretted making a particular decision must grant that his or her evaluation of the action itself or its likely effects was wrong. One example of such a mistake is buying a "lemon," a used car that looked good but turned out to be a "money pit." In the case of a used car, the best way to ascertain its goodness or badness is to ask a mechanic to examine it. Mechanics know the criteria for goodness in cars. In the case of our bodies we turn to physicians. They know the criteria to judge, for example, whether I have a mild cold or serious bronchitis or Ebola. Something analogous can be assumed to hold for our lives more generally when we step beyond the boundaries of specialized knowledge. We all have a basic understanding of when our lives are in a good or a bad condition. The efforts of philosophers who make it their central task to reflect on the human goods are nothing but attempts to clarify and systematize with some degree of reliability the criteria for judging the goodness or badness of a particular condition.

In the case of the alleged badness of someone's life, the way to proceed is to analyze the factors that lead a suicidal person to see her life as something bad. If a person is in good physical and psychological health; has a steady income, a rewarding job, a stable marriage, and well-adapted children; enjoys traveling and hiking; is full of curiosity about things near and far; retains a good sense of humor; and feels supported by her friends, it would be extremely paradoxical if she told us that her life was bad. In order to believe her we would probably have to assume that something in the overall picture has been misrepresented: perhaps her marriage is failing or her job has become insecure or her health is deteriorating. Or perhaps, whether she knows it or not, she is suffering from a psychiatric illness like depression.

In fact, we typically agree that chronic illness, physical pain, poverty and destitution, abandonment and solitude, financial or professional failure, physical disfigurement, neurosis and depression, and so on, would account for the truth of a person's claim that her life is bad. These are indeed bad things, and the fact that they must be present for a true negative evaluation shows that life, in isolation from such evils, cannot be judged to be bad. Life itself remains good, and this is why we try to cure both physical and mental illness, alleviate pain, restore finances, provide companionship, provide employment, and so on. These are rational efforts under the premoral principle of practical rationality that bids us to pursue goods and avoid evils. Life itself, even surrounded by evils, remains good. Similarly, intelligence remains good, even though having intelligence sometimes leads to painful experiences (such as learning that a close friend has betrayed you or that your beloved child has been kidnapped). Eyesight is a good, even though you may see horrific events, such as a plane hijacked by terrorists being flown into a skyscraper. Because the life of a patient remains a good even if the patient is suffering, a number of consequences follow for our moral evaluation of suicide, PAS, and voluntary euthanasia.

Suicide

There is something naturally upsetting about an action in which a person ostensibly turns against herself. It seems so unnatural for someone to do this that our first reaction when we hear someone expressing suicidal intentions or see someone making a suicidal move is to try to prevent her from carrying it out. We do this under the tacit or explicit assumption that the person must be severely depressed or otherwise psychologically disturbed, and that if stopped and duly helped, she may even be grateful that we intervened. In fact, suicidal threats are often interpreted as "a cry for help" rather than as a serious determination to end it all. Since it is difficult to claim that the decisions of severely depressed or psychologically disturbed individuals are truly autonomous, the principle of autonomy cannot be invoked and intervention to prevent them committing suicide is clearly justified. In fact, defenders of suicide have to introduce two very strong conditions to make their case plausible. They have to assume a completely autonomous individual (fully informed, acting without internal or external constraints, clearly wishing and effectively intending his death, etc.) who is, moreover, free of links and responsibilities to others who may be harmed by his death.

Does such an individual exist? Most people have links to others, however tenuous they may be, and there is a good chance that those other individuals will suffer and be negatively affected, at least by the thought that they could have done something to help prevent the suicide. If the completely isolated individual is difficult to find, it is even more difficult to establish the perfect autonomy of the act itself. We have to assume that various negative conditions are present to understand why someone might consider committing suicide, but it is precisely the presence of such conditions (mental or physical illness, poverty, solitude, etc.) that often prevents us from making truly autonomous decisions. However, let us grant that the perfectly autonomous and unencumbered suicidal individual exists, that he is neither depressed nor affected by external deprivations, and that he has no family and no friends (or least none who will be harmed by his death). What follows from this? Would his suicide be morally justified? If so, under what principle?

The principle of autonomy would only justify nonintervention by others to prevent him from committing suicide, but this tells us nothing about the morality of suicide itself. As in previous cases, we have to turn to other principles and identify the principle under which the action falls. It doubtless falls under nonmaleficence. Suicide is, after all, a narrower case of homicide—that is, of intentionally killing a human being (in this case, oneself)—and is therefore prohibited by the principle that tells us not to destroy the basic human good of life. Suicide, then, is a morally wrong type of action.

It is clear that even an allegedly autonomous suicide is a deeply irrational action not only because of the attack on the basic human good of one's life but because autonomy is turned against itself. Autonomy is exercised to end autonomy. It is a violation of autonomy to destroy autonomy, even autonomously. If autonomy is so valuable, we should not destroy it, either in ourselves or others. In this sense, freely choosing suicide is even more irrational than freely selling oneself into slavery because in the case of slavery the possibility of future freedom remains. There is, by contrast, no return from death to life.

Physician-Assisted Suicide

Physician-assisted suicide is a subset of the class of conduct we call "suicide" and is therefore to be morally judged as a narrower instance within the broader set. If suicide in general is to be considered wrong under the principle of nonmaleficence, then PAS is also morally unacceptable. The specific novelty in PAS is the intervention of a physician who provides the means for a person to bring about her own death.

The moral question to be considered is whether it is morally correct or incorrect for a physician to use his expertise in medicine to aid someone in committing suicide. Since he is not performing the main action, he should not be judged as an agent but as someone aiding someone else's action. Should he do it if asked by someone who considers her condition unbearable and wishes to take her life in an efficient and painless manner? Moreover, should he do it if he lives in a state such as Oregon, where the law allows him to assist a person to commit suicide, at least one who is "terminally ill," without fear of penalty?[2] Would he even have a moral obligation to provide assistance if there were no other physician available to do so?

These questions raise a host of broader issues that must be clarified as we proceed. First, the fact that an action is legal, insofar as it is explicitly authorized by law in a given jurisdiction, does not guarantee that it is morally right. The law should follow morality, not the other way around. In fact, the natural law view is that an unjust law, a law that violates fundamental moral principles, is in some sense not really "law" at all (despite that fact that it has been validly enacted by a legislature), just as a pharmaceutical that in fact poisons patients rather than cures them is not really a "medicine" (despite the fact it has been approved as a medicine by the relevant regulatory body). The decision of the physician must be judged morally, independently of the law in the jurisdiction where the action will be performed. History is replete with examples of people doing immoral things that were permitted by law. Think, for example, of slavery in ancient Rome or, more recently, in the United States.

Second, PAS (and also euthanasia, as we shall see) raises questions that take us from the general domain of bioethics into the domain of professional medical ethics because they affect the physician *as* physician. With the advances in medicine since the last century, the norms of medical ethics have become more complex and detailed, but this should not distract us from the essentials. Mainstream medicine as it is practiced today originated in Greece as a craft or art (*téchne* in Greek) that marshals means to attain a specific goal: the healing of the individual patient. Medicine often aims at preventing sickness and untimely death and providing comfort and alleviating suffering, especially when healing is no longer possible, but health was and still is the human good that defines the practice of medicine.

Two basic objections can be raised against this characterization of medicine. One is that the concept of "health" has been subject to skeptical criticism. One often hears that a condition that used to be considered a pathological state is no longer regarded as such, and that what was taken to be a healthy condition is now seen as defective, especially in the context of mental health. While it is true that there is room for significant and sometimes serious disagreement about what counts as "mental health" and "mentally ill," it cannot be seriously doubted that medicine continues to be practiced under the assumption of a paradigmatic notion of physical health that provides the criteria for everyday diagnosis and treatment. Physicians assume that a healthy pancreas ought to produce insulin and on that basis reach the diagnosis that a patient whose pancreas fails to produce insulin is diabetic. Practicing physicians and surgeons cannot afford to be skeptical about the notion of health.

The second objection is that, while there may be objective parameters for the determination of health, the healthy state is a good for the patient only if the patient feels that it is good for her. The unilateral determination of the good of the patient by the physician, the objection continues, is nothing but a remnant of the historical medical paternalism that modern medicine tries to overcome. Patient autonomy requires a doctor to do not what he thinks is good for the patient but what the patient wishes. The patient has the last word on what is good for her. Patient desire trumps medical opinion. This conflict seldom arises because most patients defer to the opinion of their physician. They are ready to acknowledge that he is, by training, an expert in the medical good, and they themselves consider it to be identical to their own good. Most patients are willing to take the drugs prescribed by their doctor or to undergo surgery at his recommendation. But conflicts may arise, for example, when a physician does not take into account the overall condition of a patient or when a patient requests a service that is either futile or openly inconsistent with the medical good. There is no general formula to reach a resolution of every such conflict, but it is useful to keep in mind that there are right and wrong desires, so just having a desire does not guarantee that it is of the right sort. Should a physician comply with a request for female genital mutilation or the amputation of healthy limb or to be blinded?

The request for PAS is an occasion that generates a confrontation between patient desires and medical commitment to specific goals. Under the principle of conscience, it seems unavoidable for a conscientious physician to conclude that he must abide by what he sees as the medical good, and that aiding a patient in securing her death instead of her health is inconsistent with the defining purpose of the medical profession. To characterize PAS as a form of healing or medical "treatment" (Glannon 2005, 137) is a contradiction in terms. PAS is not helping to make whole or to make well; it is helping to make dead.

In PAS a physician plays an ancillary role, but there is another practice, euthanasia, in which the doctor is the main agent.

Euthanasia

Euthanasia (a "good death") occurs when a physician intentionally ends the life of the patient, typically by administering a lethal injection, in order to put an end to the patient's suffering. The physician may perform euthanasia rather than arrange PAS because the patient is physically unable to kill herself even with assistance or because she is able to but would rather the doctor did the deed. If euthanasia is freely requested by the patient then it is "voluntary" euthanasia. If a physician intentionally causes the death of a competent patient who does not want to die, this is "involuntary" euthanasia. If the patient whose life is intentionally ended is incompetent, like a baby or a person with advanced dementia, then it is "nonvoluntary" euthanasia. Euthanasia can be brought about actively, such as by giving the patient a lethal injection, or passively, such as by withholding or withdrawing a treatment that would prevent his death. In the case of active and passive euthanasia, the intention of the physician is morally decisive. Intention here does not mean the ultimate intention, to relieve suffering, but the choice to bring about by effective means the primary goal of the action itself—namely, the death of the patient. In other words, a doctor carrying out euthanasia typically has two intentions, one (his ultimate goal) to alleviate suffering, and the second (his proximate goal, chosen and intended as means to that ultimate goal) to kill the patient. It is the latter, the intentional killing of the patient, that makes his action "euthanasia" as opposed to "the administration of palliative treatment."

In the case of "active" euthanasia, typically by the administration of a lethal poison, the agent intentionally causes death. (If he did not intend it, he would not administer the poison.) But in withholding or omitting a life-saving treatment, this is not necessarily the case. Death may be intended (and this is would be "passive" euthanasia or intentional killing carried out by deliberate omission), but it may not, although foreseen, be intended.

Euthanasia, the intentional ending of a patient's life, must be distinguished from letting the patient die. If the intention of the agent in withholding treatment is not to kill the patient but to relieve the patient of the suffering caused by a procedure that has become too painful or is ineffective, then we are dealing with a different type of conduct, an omission that is rightly described as "letting die." From a moral point of view, as we shall see, there is also a significant difference between passive euthanasia and legitimate letting die.

The moral judgment on the different kinds of euthanasia, and on letting die, will follow a similar path to the one we trod in our discussion of suicide. When a physician engages in conduct that intentionally and actively seeks the death of the patient, there is a violation of nonmaleficence. The basic human good of life is attacked. Moreover, if the patient does not wish to die, the autonomy of the individual is also violated. This explains why involuntary euthanasia is almost universally rejected: it is a practice in which two basic moral principles are simultaneously violated. But does the fact that someone autonomously wishes to be deprived of the good of life make it morally permissible for the physician to comply with her wishes? Once again we encounter the limits of autonomy. Autonomy, as we have argued, does not guarantee morally right action. The physician must govern his actions primarily by the principles of beneficence and nonmaleficence. And in the presence of acute pain and suffering, these principles enjoin, first, medical treatment and, second, effective palliative care when recovery is no longer possible. The point is to attack what is bad in the condition of the patient (the illness and the pain, but not her life) and to let her die as peacefully as possible.

There are, moreover, real concerns that if the law were to allow voluntary euthanasia or physician-assisted suicide, it would lead down a "slippery slope" to ending the lives of patients who did not autonomously request a hastened death, who were not suffering seriously, or for whom there were alternatives such as palliative care (Keown 2002). There are two "slippery slope" arguments. The first, the "empirical" argument, runs that it would not be possible effectively to control the practice. How is the law to define concepts like "unacceptable suffering," and how is it to ensure that requests are truly autonomous, and not the result of clinical depression or pressure, subtle or otherwise, from relatives? The second, the "logical" argument, runs that if it is ethical to end the life of a suffering patient who requests it, it is logically ethical to end the life of a suffering patient who cannot. If voluntary euthanasia is justified by autonomy and beneficence (which, of course, natural law ethics denies), why does beneficence not justify euthanasia of the incompetent? Why withhold relief simply because they cannot request it?

Let us turn now to two possible scenarios that tend to blur the line that divides legitimate letting die from euthanasia. The first is the employment of strong pain-relieving drugs that may have the incidental effect of hastening death. The second is the withdrawing of life-sustaining means. In resolving questions of the first kind, the mainstream tradition in Western ethics has developed the principle of double effect (PDE), and in resolving questions of the second kind, it has introduced the distinction between a "proportionate" treatment and a "disproportionate" treatment.

Double-Effect Reasoning

We explained the PDE and its possible application to the removal of the unborn child in the previous chapter. Because of its importance in natural law ethical theory, let us remind ourselves of the principle's standard formulation. An action that has a good and a bad effect is morally permissible if and only if the following conditions are satisfied:

(1) The action itself is not morally incorrect—that is, it does not violate by itself any moral norm and ultimately the principles of beneficence and nonmaleficence;

(2) The good effect intended by the agent is not achieved through the bad effect;

(3) The bad effect is not intended by the agent but only foreseen and tolerated; and

(4) There is proportionality between the good effect and the bad one. If the good effect is minimal and the bad effect considerable, the action may well be wrong. Moreover, if there is an alternative

course of action that does not involve producing the bad effect, that course should be followed.

Just as we considered a standard example of the application of the principle at the beginning of life (in the case of Tiffany, the pregnant woman with a cancerous uterus), we can consider a standard example in relation to the end of life.

Roger is days from death and in considerable pain. He asks his doctor, Dr. Shah, if she can do anything to alleviate his pain. Dr. Shah replies that she can administer an analgesic, morphine, in order to ease his pain but that there is a risk that it may also have the effect of shortening his life by a few hours. May the doctor administer the morphine with Roger's consent even though she knows it will have the effect of shortening his life?

According to the PDE, the answer is in the affirmative. Dr. Shah would be acting ethically because (1) to provide an analgesic is a morally permissible action; (2) the alleviation of the pain is not achieved through Roger's death but by means of the morphine (his pain is relieved whether or not his death is hastened); (3) Dr. Shah does not intend Roger's death (it is assumed) but merely foresees it (if she did intend his death, the PDE would not apply: neither its first nor third condition would be satisfied); and (4) the alleviation of Roger's acute pain is not out of proportion to the shortening of his life by a few hours or days. (If, by contrast, Roger's pain were slight and the shortening of his life as a result of the morphine were considerable, the good and the bad would be disproportionate and the action immoral. Moreover, if there were an equally effective palliative drug that Dr. Shah could use that would not have the effect of hastening death, she would not be justified in using the life-shortening drug.) In other words, if all the conditions spelled out by the PDE have been satisfied, the bad outcome, the incidental shortening of the life of a patient, is not in violation of nonmaleficence. (Although ours is a standard hypothetical used to illustrate the application of the PDE at the end of life, the administration of morphine in proper doses at the end of life does not, in fact, shorten life.) This is, however, entirely different from euthanasia, where the intention of the doctor—in administering what may be exactly the same dose—is precisely to shorten the life of the patient. The difference between ethical palliative care and euthanasia is sometimes tersely expressed as the difference between "killing the pain" and "killing the patient." But, it might be asked, could a doctor who performs euthanasia not claim that his intention is merely to "kill the pain," just like Dr. Shah's intention? No. The doctor who performs euthanasia may very well intend to ease pain, but he also intends to kill the patient, as a means of ending the pain.

Let us now turn to the ethical question of when it is ethical to withhold or withdraw medical treatment or tube feeding.

Proportionate and Disproportionate Treatments

It is both rational and morally right (under the principle of beneficence) to preserve one's own life. It is also both rational and morally obligatory for a physician to do her best to preserve the lives of her patients, and yet she knows that a time may come when there is nothing further she can do to prevent or postpone death. There are cases, however, when something can indeed be done because the illness or the pathological condition is not imminently fatal. Several options are open to the physician. She can do nothing, thus omitting a crucial intervention, with the intention that the patient die. This would be passive euthanasia. At the opposite extreme is the marshaling of all available means to keep the patient alive at all costs. This is often called "medical obstinacy" or "vitalism," which can be interpreted as an irrational and ultimately futile struggle against death itself. Somewhere in between is to allow the causal factor to run its course and thus let the patient die, foreseeing yet not intending his death.

Since the sixteenth century efforts have been made to develop objective criteria to decide whether a decision to withhold or withdraw treatment is morally correct. This is important because of the need to pass public moral judgment on the actions of health care providers who may do something wrong even while having the best of intentions. A physician may well not intend the death of a particular patient (and hence be not guilty of engaging in euthanasia), and yet if she lets him die in certain circumstances there may be a failure of beneficence on her part. From the perspective of the conscientious patient there is also the question whether rejecting certain forms of treatment would constitute suicidal behavior. An obsessive patient or his family, on the other hand, may accuse a doctor of negligent behavior for not doing enough on his behalf.

Considerations such as these led to the development of the distinction between "proportionate" treatment and "disproportionate" treatment. There have been variations in the terminology employed. Historically, the distinction was between "ordinary" and "extraordinary" treatments. However, sometimes the mistake was made of interpreting "ordinary" and "extraordinary" in their everyday sense of "frequently employed" and "seldom employed." But the distinction we are concerned with is a moral one, not an empirical one. It concerns what doctors ought to provide, not what they in fact usually provide. In order to avoid slipping into this error, many bioethicists today prefer to talk about "proportionate" and "disproportionate" treatments. Despite the difference in terminology, the basis for the distinction remains the same. It provides a criterion to pass moral judgment on different forms of medical treatment. The use of proportionate treatment is ethically obligatory, whereas the use of disproportionate treatment is ethically optional.

The crucial question, of course, is how to distinguish between proportionate and disproportionate treatments. Although through the centuries different authors have provided slightly different accounts, the mainstream natural law position (one that, like the PDE, has influenced professional medical ethics) has been that, in drawing the distinction, one should consider the burdens (physical, psychological, financial, etc.) imposed by the treatment and the benefits of the treatment. Both the burdens and the benefits are to be judged with reference to the individual patient. In other words, the moral question is: Would this treatment, even if it offers significant benefits, be too burdensome to the patient? Take Constance. Constance has been diagnosed with cancer of the bowel. Her doctor suggests chemotherapy. Even if the chemotherapy offers a reasonable chance of remission, if it nevertheless causes excessive burdens to Constance in terms of serious, persistent pain and nausea, Constance has a sound ethical reason for refusing the treatment. Sometimes the treatment can be worse than the disease. Excessive burden is therefore a sound ethical reason for refusing treatment, even treatment that offers a reasonable prospect of preserving life or restoring health. Another sound ethical reason for refusing a proposed treatment is if the treatment offers no reasonable prospect of benefit. If the doctor says to Constance, "I'm afraid that chemotherapy will offer only a one in ten million chance of curing your cancer," Constance may reasonably refuse the treatment on the ground that it would be futile.[3] In short, there can be no moral duty to consent to a treatment that is futile or that, if not futile, will involve excessive burden.

In the distant past, before the development of anesthesia, the amputation of a diseased limb could reasonably be considered disproportionate because of the pain involved in the surgery, particularly if the patient was highly sensitive to pain. Given advances in surgery, not least anesthetics and antiseptics, it would be much more difficult today to classify amputation as disproportionate.

Problems arise symmetrically when a physician either decides not to apply a proportionate treatment or insists on continuing with a disproportionate treatment. Likewise, a patient (or his family or proxy) sometimes rejects a proportionate treatment or requests that a disproportionate treatment be continued. There is no mathematical formula to resolve such problems but only general ethical considerations that may be useful to guide the corresponding deliberations of doctor, patient, and proxy.

A doctor who fails to apply an available treatment that would not be unduly burdensome (not too painful, or too expensive, etc.) and moreover would be effective may be rightly accused of negligence, or worse. Equally, a doctor who insists on continuing a treatment that causes excessive suffering and has become futile may produce harm, and has an ethical obligation to desist. From the perspective of the patient, things are not as clear-cut because the distinction itself is relative to the condition of the patient. Refusal of a cheap and effective drug may be suicidal, motivated by an intention to put an end to life: think of a diabetic who refuses his regular insulin shot because he is bored with life. Such refusals are seriously immoral. But a refusal of treatment may be, alternatively, a legitimate rejection of a means that the patient judges to be disproportionate from the broader perspective of his personal good. The medical good sought could be rightly regarded as only a part of his overall well-being. And, conversely, consent to a very painful treatment may be motivated by personal courage and the hope to live long enough to achieve other, nonmedical goals (such as to see a long estranged son, to celebrate the wedding of a daughter, or the birth of a new grandson, etc.) Decisions regarding the use or rejection of proportionate and disproportionate treatments in particular cases will be the result of a host of variables considered in light of the more general principles. Ideally such decisions should be the result of discussion between the attending physician and the patient (or the patient's proxy). Much will depend on the particular patient and his or her personal situation, something physicians ought to appreciate and respect.

One question that has generated much media attention and bioethical debate concerns the question whether there is a duty to tube-feed patients in a persistent vegetative state (PVS). Is this a proportionate or a disproportionate treatment? Is it a medical treatment at all?

Tube Feeding Patients in PVS

Even though PVS is not common, the medically assisted nutrition and hydration, or tube feeding, of patients in PVS deserves scrutiny because it has become an issue of worldwide controversy. The controversy has been sparked by highly publicized cases like that of Terri Schiavo in the United States,[4] Eluana Englaro in Italy (Day 2009), and Tony Bland in England.[5] In all three cases withdrawal of tube feeding was permitted by courts. All three patients died shortly—though by no means promptly—after its withdrawal. Were these cases, on the one hand, of passive euthanasia or, on the other, of legitimate letting die? Without being privy to all of the particular circumstances surrounding each of these cases, not least the intentions of those who withdrew or ordered the withdrawal of tube feeding, it is difficult to reach a responsible answer to this moral question, so our aim will be to set out the more general considerations supporting each side of the controversy. Natural law ethicists can be found on either side.

Before describing PVS and discussing the ethics of withholding or withdrawing tube feeding in such cases, we should pause to note the importance of the words we use, words that can be quite loaded. When discussing abortion in the previous chapter we noted the different resonances of the words "fetus" and "child." Here too we should note the different resonances of, on the one hand, "medically assisted, or artificial, nutrition and hydration" and, on the other hand, "tube feeding." The former connotes a medical intervention by doctors in white coats in hospitals. The latter, not so. Some relatives care for their loved ones in PVS and similar conditions at home, and feed them by tube. While it is true that some issues in bioethics have been raised by new developments in medical technology, feeding tubes, even if "technology," are hardly new. Equally, it is one thing to talk about a patient in PVS. It is quite another to talk about a patient in a state of persistent wakefulness without awareness. The former invites the conceptualization of the patient not as a human person, but as a "vegetable." Indeed, it is not rare to hear people (heartlessly) describe those with such profound mental disabilities as "cabbages."

PVS is a condition that involves the loss of functioning of the cerebral cortex, which is necessary for the higher functions of the brain. A patient in PVS is thought to be completely unaware of herself and her surroundings, unable to perceive light, sounds, smells, and so on. Together with the loss of perception, a patient in PVS is also thought to have lost the sensations connected with perception, notably the ability to feel pain. Finally, loss of cortical activity also entails the loss of the ability for thought, action, and communication with other human beings. However, since the remainder of the brain remains functioning, a person in PVS breathes unaided, has a beating heart, and can digest and excrete. Patients in PVS may have lost the ability to swallow. In short, PVS is rather like being in a persistent coma but, unlike a coma, the patient has sleep–wake cycles. Patients in PVS are not, as some journalists seem to think, "brain dead" (a condition we will discuss later), "terminally ill," or dependent on mechanical ventilators. Provided that patients in PVS are fed and their infections are treated with antibiotics, they can often live, without machines, for many years.

Tube feeding is designed to overcome the obstacle posed by a PVS patient's inability to swallow (or, if the patient has not lost that ability, to make it easier for the staff to feed them, both in terms of time and to reduce the risk of food going down the wrong way). It consists either of the insertion of a plastic tube through the nose and down the esophagus directly into the stomach (a nasogastric tube) or of the surgical insertion of a tube through the abdomen into the stomach (a gastrostomy tube). In both cases the nutrients have to be prescribed by a physician or a similar expert, and both kinds of tube can result in infections and other injuries.

Different views of patients in PVS have been proposed:

(1) As we shall see in the next chapter, some have proposed to make

the loss of all higher brain function a criterion for the death of the individual. On this view, an individual in PVS should be declared dead. Her organs could be lawfully extracted for transplantation, and she could be buried. This view, however, flies in the face of the biological evidence. Patients in PVS continue to breathe and metabolize nutrients, exhibit homeostasis, and so on. In fact, the ethical controversy arises because Terri, Eluana, and Tony were not dead in the normal sense of the word when they fell into PVS, and in fact died only some years later after their tube feeding was stopped.

(2) Some would agree that a patient in PVS is alive but hold that only her body continues to live. The "person" herself passed away the moment the loss of the higher human functions became irreversible. This view requires us to posit two deaths, one of the "person" and one of the "body," and is only possible on the basis of the sort of dualistic view we considered in chapter 4. Only two substances capable of independent existence can be destroyed at different points in time. Since the mind, the substance that dualists identify with the person, has ceased to function, adherents of this view argue that the patient in PVS does not possess intrinsic dignity and need not be respected in the way we respect those who are fully conscious. A PVS patient is, as one advocate of this viewpoint put it, a "manicured vegetable" (Dworkin 1994, 192). This interpretation of the condition of a patient in PVS stands or falls with the plausibility of substance dualism, which we considered and rejected earlier.

(3) The monist view of our nature takes the PVS patient to be an individual who is alive and exercising his basic biological powers but who has lost the active use of sentience and thought due to incapacitation of the organs necessary for those functions. Does this loss of function entail the loss of personhood? Since personhood, on the monist view, does not reside in a substance externally attached to or occupying the body but is an essential power deeply rooted in our biology (we exercise reason because we grow to have the organs that sustain the higher functions), it follows that the loss of the actualization of the higher functions (without the loss of life) does not mean that personhood is lost.

Oedipus could not see because he destroyed his eyes, but he did not lose the root power of sight. If medical technology made it possible, say, to take his stem cells, grow new eyes, and reconnect them to his brain, he would be able to see again. By analogy we can assume that if the neocortical part of the brain of a patient in PVS could be properly repaired, again perhaps by using the patient's own stem cells, he could in principle regain awareness and other higher functions. It is thus reasonable to hold that a patient in PVS continues to be a person, though a severely disabled person. The genetic program that governs his existence as a unified organism still includes the information leading to the support of thought, even though that information is contingently inactive. A PVS patient is thus worthy of the same respect due all other persons.

Consider also the implications of views (1) and (2) not only for those in PVS but also for human beings with other mental disabilities. There are reportedly over 40 million people worldwide with dementia.[6] Should they (at least if their dementia is sufficiently advanced that they have lost their higher mental abilities like self-consciousness) be certified (on view 1) as "dead" or (on view 2) as "vegetables"? On either view, would it be unethical (at least painlessly and with the approval of their relatives, if any) to use them for experimentation (even lethal) or to take their organs (even vital)? And, if they are not to be used for experimentation or organ harvesting, would it be unethical to dispose of them the way we standardly dispose of the dead, by burial or cremation (at least if—to ensure they did not suffer, and for aesthetic reasons—their heartbeat and respiration was first stopped)?

If views (1) and (2) of the condition of a patient in PVS were correct, there would be no problem about withdrawing tube feeding. On the first view the patient is already dead, and on the second view the "person" is dead. Why would it be wrong to stop nutrition and hydration of a cadaver or a residual body? It is only on interpretation (3) that a difficult moral dilemma arises. Let us assume first that the person, long before falling into PVS, had left clear instructions (in an advance directive) that she did not want to be fed by tube if she were ever in PVS. That her wish be respected would be urged by those who advocate a "right to die." However, this vague phrase needs careful analysis. We should not turn a deaf ear to its paradoxical sound. Consider "the right to be mugged." This sounds absurd simply because it is bad to be mugged and our common understanding is that a right is basically a legitimate claim to something good. As we saw earlier, a conceptual analysis of the alleged badness of certain lives shows that it is not life itself that is bad but certain evils that happen to affect it in certain circumstances, like pain or disease. For living beings, death remains, on a physical level, the ultimate bad. This helps to explain why many people go to great lengths to safeguard their life and health (from avoiding danger to taking regular exercise and eating healthy foods). So, if the "right to die" means a right to end one's life, to commit suicide by refusing life-prolonging treatment, it should be rejected. Or does the phrase connote a right to resist medical obstinacy or vitalism? Does it mean a right to resist doctors who, forgetful that the core purpose of medicine is to restore patients to health, practice "meddlesome medicine" and try to preserve life at all costs, even by way of clearly disproportionate treatments that impose excessive burdens on the patient or her family? If this is what the "right to die" means, it is a legitimate right. (However, the dangerous ambiguity in the phrase is a good reason for avoiding its use altogether.)

An autonomous decision to decline tube feeding can, then, be interpreted in a manner that squares with practical rationality. It may well be a choice to avoid a disproportionate burden on oneself and one's family (such as the considerable expense of being cared for around the clock in a private facility) or charitably to save health care resources so that they can be used to benefit others even though one foresees that the result of refusing tube feeding will be death. If either of these reasons accounts for the refusal, it seems reasonable to honor the choice of the patient.

But what if the patient has not made an advance directive refusing treatment or has not appointed a proxy with authority to refuse on her behalf? The question whether to institute or to continue tube feeding in such a case is difficult. Even among natural law ethicists who agree about the basic goodness of life and about the importance of due respect for the person in PVS, there are two different positions:

(A) Those who adopt the first position favor a narrow application of the distinction between "proportionate" and "disproportionate" treatments. Focusing on the means involved in tube feeding, they argue that tube feeding is not a treatment at all—it is simply basic care, like keeping the patient warm and clean; that delivering the nutrients is neither painful nor excessively burdensome; and that it is not futile because it keeps the patient alive for as long as he can assimilate the nutrients. On this approach tube feeding turns out to be a proportionate means for virtually every patient. Withholding tube feeding from a patient in PVS, or withdrawing it from such a patient, involves the intentional ending of the patient's life or at least the intentional abandonment of the patient. The rock-bottom moral conviction sustaining this position is that providing bread and water to a fellow human being, especially when sick and vulnerable, is such an elementary duty that the fact that they are delivered through a tube is irrelevant. Others may object that in a disadvantaged area where the required technological means are not available, those patients would have naturally passed away under the effects of their pathology. Defenders of position (A) would reply that where insulin is not available, diabetics die, but that this is not a valid reason to withhold insulin treatment if it is available.

(B) Those adopting the second position favor a contextual application of the distinction between "proportionate" and "disproportionate" means. They broaden the scope of what is to be considered in drawing the distinction. They accept that tube feeding is not therapy (what, after all, is it thought to be treating?) but hold that it nevertheless requires medical expertise; that although the delivery of the nutrients is not excessively burdensome for the patient, the care of the PVS patient can be very burdensome (psychologically and financially) for the family and the community; and that there is a sense of futility in keeping an unconscious patient alive, with no hope of recovery, for five, fifteen, or fifty or more years only because there is a technologically advanced way of providing nutrients. For these reasons, tube feeding can be considered disproportionate for certain patients, and its withdrawal would amount to legitimate letting die. The grounding intuition behind this position is that modern medical technology is leading us to needlessly prolong lives, and we do not have the conceptual resources to justify a rejection of its use. In fact, modern medical technology is guided by exactly the same criteria that characterize proportionate treatments: its goal is to discover procedures, instruments, drugs, and so on that are less and less burdensome and more and more efficient. In other words, modern medical technology, on this second view, tends to turn all means into proportionate means and thus generates a drive toward the relentless use of all successful procedures available to the physician. Medical obstinacy is not simply an arbitrary choice of some doctors: it is deeply rooted in a pervasive feature of contemporary culture. According to this view, we owe it to our weak and vulnerable fellow human beings to protect them from a technologically driven prolongation of their lives. Of course, those adopting position (A) could counter that this is not really a matter of new technological development at all, that tube feeding is a fairly basic way of facilitating the feeding of patients who can no longer swallow, or those who can.

More collective thought by ethicists in the natural law tradition will be needed before a consensus is reached on the question whether there is a duty to tube-feed patients in PVS. The natural law tradition is a living, developing tradition. It does not pretend to have reached a consensus on all the answers.

A final point. The practical importance of the question should not be overstated. Patients in PVS often contract infections, not least due to their immobile condition and to the placing and replacing of the tube. The question whether antibiotics may ethically be withheld when PVS patients contract infections would probably attract a substantial consensus in favor of an affirmative answer. Antibiotics are indubitably a medical treatment rather than basic care, and it is much easier to argue that they are a disproportionate treatment in the case of patients in PVS. If the core goal of medicine is to restore patients to health and well-functioning, or to some approximation to it, then, given the unarguably deprived condition in which patients in reliably diagnosed PVS find themselves, a condition of profoundly diminished flourishing, and given the (present) inability of medical science to restore them to a condition approximating health and well-functioning, there is a good ethical argument that antibiotics in such a case constitute futile medical treatment. Giving antibiotics to a patient in PVS is, the argument would run, similar to ventilating someone who is near death. Neither can restore the patient to health. Both are futile. Neither is, therefore, morally required.

Notes

1. This chapter could profitably be read in conjunction with Gómez-Lobo (2002, chap. 8). The debate over physician-assisted suicide and euthanasia has generated an enormous literature. See, for example, Jackson and Keown (2011).

2. See the Death with Dignity Act, *Oregon.gov*, October 27, 1997, http://public .health.oregon.gov/ProviderPartnerResources/EvaluationResearch/Deathwith DignityAct/Pages/index.aspx.

3. The word "futile" comes from the Latin for "leaky." Futile means ineffective or pointless, like trying to fill a leaky bucket with water.

4. See "Brain-Damaged Terri Schiavo Dies," BBC, March 31, 2005, http:// news.bbc.co.uk/2/hi/americas/4398131.stm. For a revealing legal analysis of the case, see Snead (2005).

5. For an ethical and legal analysis of the declaration by the Law Lords that it was lawful to withdraw his tube-feeding see Keown (1997).

6. In 2013 there were an estimated 44.4 million people worldwide with dementia. This number is predicted to increase to an estimated 75.6 million in 2030, and 135.5 million in 2050. Alzheimer's Disease International, "Dementia Statistics," http://www.alz.co.uk/research/statistics.

Chapter 8
ISSUES IN TRANSPLANTATION

Medical technology is morally neutral: it can be used ethically or un-ethically. It is sometimes used unethically, to take life. Another unethical application is in the futile and wasteful attempt to preserve life at all costs. But technology can also be used for good purposes. Organ transplantation, for example, has restored many patients to normal functioning, including many patients who would otherwise have died because of the failure of a vital organ like a heart or liver. Organ transplantation is clearly in line with the traditional goals of medicine: it aims at the restoration of health and the prevention of untimely death. But, until scientists are able to create organs in the laboratory, transplants require that a human organ be removed, either from a dead donor or, in the case of paired organs like kidneys, from a living donor. A host of ethical questions arise with regard to the choices made and the actions performed by the many agents involved in transplantation procedures. Let us consider just a few of those questions.

The "Dead-Donor Rule"

The admirable success of transplantation techniques has given hope to thousands of patients who a few decades ago would have given up hope. In many developed countries, such patients can now be placed on a waiting list for an organ. This has generated a sizeable demand for organs, with supply noticeably lagging behind. There are various reasons why organs are not donated in sufficient numbers, and it is the task of social scientists to determine the reasons for this through empirical research. Moral philosophy, as a normative discipline, is not called upon to explain collective behavior but to ethically assess any proposals put forward to improve the availability of organs. One proposal is to enact "presumed consent" laws, which would allow organs to be taken after death unless the deceased had registered an objection during his or her lifetime. Another proposal is to create a commercial market in organs. Yet another proposal, and one we shall consider here, is to allow the removal of vital organs (such as a heart) even though the donor is not yet dead.

If we ignore living donation (e.g., a kidney given by a brother to a sister), the process of organ transplantation usually originates when someone is involved in a serious accident, for example, a motorcycle accident, and his organs are removed, preserved, transported to a transplantation center, and grafted into the body of a recipient. If the extraction team waits too long, the viability of the organs may be compromised due to loss of oxygenation.

Sometimes the donor is in a hospital setting and has agreed to donate her organs, but the likely circumstances of her death may lead to loss of oxygenation and make the use of her organs infeasible. To deal with such cases, and in order to increase supply, some have proposed extracting organs from patients who, though still alive, are close to death and have previously agreed to donation. The acceptance of such a practice would amount to abandoning the so-called dead-donor rule, the moral norm requiring that the removal of vital organs take place only after the donor has died. If the donor is still alive, taking her vital organs inevitably brings about her death. Is abandoning the dead-donor rule morally justifiable? A utilitarian justification based on promoting the happiness of those receiving the organs might be advanced. However, for reasons given earlier, utilitarianism was rejected as ethically unacceptable. And, even if the donor had consented to the removal of a vital organ, would its removal not be a case of using one human being as a mere means for the benefit of another? Such concerns may lead opponents of the dead-donor rule to switch their focus to the process of organ extraction itself and argue either that the resulting death is a form of justified active euthanasia or that, if one accepts the PDE, it is a case in which the death of the donor is a foreseen but unintended consequence of the extraction and which satisfies the PDE (DeGrazia 2005, 154–55, esp. n85). Both lines of argument are misguided.

Even if active euthanasia were morally right (which, as we maintained earlier, it is not), killing a human being for the benefit of other individuals could hardly count as euthanasia, for a central element in the concept of euthanasia is benefit to the patient herself. Killing one person by taking their organs to benefit others is not "euthanasia" in any recognizable meaning of the term.

The suggestion that the PDE might justify the rejection of the dead-donor rule is also unpersuasive. John Finnis, considering a comparable scenario in which a hypothetical eccentric surgeon, while operating on a patient for appendicitis, removes the patient's heart for the purpose of later experimentation, comments that the surgeon treats the patient's body as his own to dispose of and that, though the surgeon's intent is not precisely to kill the patient, it is precisely to treat the patient as if he were a mere subhuman object. The removal of the heart is, moreover, an intentional mutilation, a violation of the patient's bodily integrity as a means. (Finnis 2011a, 193–94; 196–97n3).

Further, abandoning the dead-donor rule in order to increase the availability of organs for transplantation may backfire. If practice changed to allow organs to be taken from those who were not yet dead, many reasonable people would surely refuse to register as organ donors, or would refuse permission for the organs of their loved ones to be used, for fear that their organs would be harvested while they are still alive and while they perhaps had a chance of survival. The loss of trust generated by those fears would also have lasting consequences for the medical profession itself, a profession whose social standing and ability to carry out its role of preserving life and restoring health depend on its uncompromised commitment to the life and health of each patient. On both moral and prudential grounds, then, it would be wrong to abandon the dead-donor rule. To observe the rule, however, we must determine when someone has indeed died.

The Determination of Death

When has a human being died? The answer is not as simple as the question. Before considering answers that have been given, it would be useful to clarify what has become a very convoluted and controversial issue. The determination of the death of a human being should be considered against the background of at least the following assumptions:

(1) We know that death is something that eventually happens to all living organisms: plants, animals, and humans. Inorganic things like plastic ducks do not die, and human beings as a subset of living beings do not undergo a biologically special kind of death.

(2) There is only one death for each organism. To assign more than one death to an organism entails that the given organism did not die the first time or that we are dealing with more than one organism.

(3) Death is an event in nature, and the determination of death is an objective judgment on our part. To say that the determination of death is "a moral issue" is to confuse two quite different human actions. Our decision to do or not to do something (e.g., to remove organs) is subject to moral evaluation, but the determination that a human being is dead is not a moral issue (though it may have moral implications for how we should act, or not act, in the light of that determination). The determination of death can be correct or incorrect, accurate or inaccurate, but it cannot be morally right or morally wrong.

To hold that death is an event in nature that has to be objectively ascertained does not entail that it is easy to verify when it has taken place or that it can be subject to direct observation. Indeed, in past decades there has been a significant change in the way death may be determined. Some authors talk about a change in the "definition" of death and are willing to enumerate multiple "definitions" among which individuals may choose. But this seems clearly wrong. To define is to assign a meaning to a term. If there is a change in definition, that is, if during a debate or conversation a new meaning is introduced for a given term or expression, those who use that term in the old sense and those who use it in the new sense may well be talking about different things. If "death" undergoes a change in definition, it becomes ambiguous, and a rational discussion about death simply cannot take place because the word stands for different things. For the sake of sound bioethical reasoning, the ordinary meaning of "death" must remain stable and should apply, as we mentioned earlier, not just to humans but also to animals, insects, trees, and plants. A simple, standard definition of death is the irreversible cessation of the life of an organism. It is true that we also talk about the death of an organ or the death of a tissue, but it is clear that these are derivative uses that can be paraphrased by using the terms "dysfunction" or "failure." Death of the brain can be correctly called "brain dysfunction" or "brain failure" by analogy with our talk about heart or liver failure. The ordinary meaning of "death," moreover, indicates that death is a negative notion. It amounts to a privation (what Aristotle called a *stéresis* [*Physics* I. 7. 191 a 7–14]). Hence, the primitive notion on which the understanding of death hinges is that of life. Stones are not deprived of life, for they were never alive in the first place.

In an ideal world we would be able to identify the essential formula of life just as we identify H_2O as the essence of water, but we are far from being able to achieve that, although it is fair to say that genetics is moving in that direction. The best we can do at present is to rely on certain signs that indicate that something is alive. For example, if a body exhibits order, nutrition and excretion, growth and development, cell division, homeostasis, and so on, we can say with confidence that it is alive (Campbell and Reece 2002, 5). If it no longer exhibits some or most of those functions, for example, cell division and growth (and if it previously did), we can presume that the organism has died. Tests, in turn, are designed to verify signs. To focus on certain signs and to neglect others in order to determine whether an organism is dead or alive is to choose a criterion. (A criterion, as its Greek root suggests, functions in the manner of a sieve that allows us to separate liquids from solids. To have a criterion for something is to possess a way of discriminating between it and items from which we want distinguish it.) Signs are naturally given, whereas criteria are chosen. To say that a criterion for embryonic death is that its cells (blastomeres) no longer divide is to decide to take cell division as a sign of life at the embryonic stage.

If we now concentrate our focus on human beings, there are three competing criteria to distinguish between a living and a dead individual. The traditional criterion has been irreversible cardiac and pulmonary arrest. To verify this criterion, various tests have been devised. Some are simple, such as placing a mirror by the patient's nose and mouth to observe condensation, and some are more sophisticated, such as listening to the heart with a stethoscope. The criterion assumes that a heartbeat (with the consequent circulation of blood) and breathing (with the consequent intake of oxygen) are basic signs of life such that their irreversible cessation indicates that death has taken place. The loss of circulatory and respiratory functions, it should be emphasized, is neither a "definition" of death nor (presumably) death itself.

With the advent of the artificial ventilator in the 1960s, the functions of the heart and lungs that would have naturally stopped as a consequence of the loss of brain function could be artificially sustained. This encouraged the search for a new criterion in the realization that heartbeat and breathing were no longer reliable signs or indicators that a person is alive since it had become possible, by way of machines, to artificially maintain these functions.

In order to discern whether somebody connected to a ventilator was dead or alive, a second and novel criterion was developed on the basis of two assumptions. The first was that the integration of biological functions is an essential aspect of life. The other assumption was that the brain is responsible for the integration of the whole organism. Under these assumptions, the complete loss of brain function was adopted as a criterion known as the "whole brain" definition of death. This criterion allows for the removal of organs of someone who is "brain dead," someone whose brain has completely ceased to function. Since this is compatible with artificially maintained breathing and heartbeat, this criterion provides favorable conditions for the extraction of oxygenated organs suitable for transplantation. In fact, the development of this criterion was arguably prompted by the progress of transplantation surgery and has been the basis of statutes regulating organ transplantation in the United States and in other countries. (Interestingly, in the United Kingdom the definition adopted by the medical profession is different: it is death of part of the brain, the "brain stem," the part of the brain that is connected to the spinal cord. It appears, then, that you could at the same time be regarded as dead by physicians in the United Kingdom but not by physicians in the United States.)

The "whole brain" criterion of death, however, has been attacked on two fronts. On one front are those who appeal to empirical evidence that is claimed to show that some patients continue to exhibit integration and integrated functioning even after they have been declared "brain dead," about which more later. The second front questions the assumption that biological integration is necessary and sufficient for human life. On the view of these critics, what matters is not bodily integration but the integration of the mind and body. Accordingly, they have proposed a different criterion, to which we shall now turn.

This third criterion holds that a human individual is dead when there is irreversible loss of all higher brain functions (Veatch 2005). Among those functions are consciousness and self-consciousness, the capacity to judge and reason, and the power to will and decide. It is known that the cortex or "higher brain" is necessary to sustain these functions. On this third criterion, once these functions are lost because the cerebral cortex has ceased to function, no human individual continues to exist, although a body with a spontaneously beating heart and unassisted breathing may continue to live. Patients in PVS would be held to satisfy this third criterion.

This higher brain criterion is, however, vulnerable to criticism (De-

Grazia, 2005, chap. 4). It is, indeed, the least reasonable of the answers we have considered to the question of when a human being has died. First, it seems to provide a criterion valid only for human beings. As we have already pointed out, death is a phenomenon that affects all living beings, including human beings, cats, and frogs. Further, it seems to defy the natural signs of life, for it allows us to declare dead an organism that may be discharging the basic functions of respiration, nutrition, excretion, growth, homeostasis, and so on—an organism that is definitely not undergoing putrefaction. Indeed, the higher brain criterion forces us to posit two deaths possibly occurring at different dates, one for the mind and a second for the body (Glannon 2005, 122). It is not surprising that no jurisdiction in the world appears to have made this criterion its legal definition of death.

From a philosophical perspective, it clear that the higher brain criterion depends on a dualistic view of human nature. If we are composites of two different things, a body and a mind (which may or may not be considered identical to our brain), and if we as persons are identical to our minds, then it is sensible to hold that when our mental powers are irretrievably lost, we have ceased to exist, independently of what may happen to our bodies. Moreover, since, on this approach, harm is equivalent to conscious harm, the living body of a permanently unconscious individual would not be harmed if its organs were extracted. On this view our bodies are extraneous to us. They are not us; they are instruments we "inhabit" and use.

The first two criteria to determine death, on the other hand, are consistent with a unified conception of human nature, with the monist view. If we are but one living being, then just as we come into being only once, we die only once, and that happens when our bodily life comes to an end, not just when we have lost consciousness. The loss of consciousness is not the destruction of a second substance but the loss of a natural power that depends on healthy brain functioning for its exercise, akin to the loss of sight through damage to the eyes or retina. It is a power we would have were it not the case that our cortex had been seriously damaged, just as serious damage to the eyes or retina leads to loss of sight. We retain both those powers even though we cannot exercise them because of the failure of the organs associated with them. As we suggested earlier, repair of someone's eyes could help them to recover vision. So too, repair of someone's cortex could help them to recover consciousness. Once they had recovered consciousness, would we say they had "come back from the dead?" Of course not. They were alive all along but had simply been unable to exercise their radical capacity for consciousness, the root capacity they had from their very beginning. They would be able to exercise their consciousness again because it was a capacity they had never lost.

Before we considered the third or neocortical criterion of death, we mentioned a challenge to the whole brain death criterion. This challenge invokes empirical evidence that is claimed to show that some patients whose brain has completely ceased to function nevertheless continue to exhibit signs of life. In order to dismiss this challenge, it would have to be shown either that the diagnosis of brain dysfunction was wrong in those cases or that the signs of life are those of lingering subsystems and not of the body as a whole.[1] Proponents of the challenge have marshaled interesting empirical evidence that they claim proves both the reliability of the diagnosis of whole brain death in virtually all cases and the holistic character of the vital functions (i.e., proportional growth, homeostasis, overall immune reaction) observed in these patients (Shewmon 1998, 2001, 2011). This challenges the view that the brain is in fact the regulator of the body's integration and suggests that the source of integration may be diffused through the body. In support of this view, it could be pointed out that a healthy embryo displays a high level of physiological coordination and integration long before he or she has a functioning brain. Perhaps, then, the integrative function is exercised not by a specific organ but by the genetic information that is at work in our bodies throughout our lives. On this view, death occurs when the overall genetic activation and coordination ceases.

On the other hand, it could be argued that an embryo is a much smaller and simpler entity than an adult human being, and the fact that embryonic self-integration does not require a brain does not entail that self-integration at later stages does not require a brain. Moreover, we do not in any event have a way of testing or observing when overall genetic activation and coordination ceases and are thus limited once again to the evidence provided by irreversible cessation of cardiopulmonary function. This appears to provide the most reliable criterion to determine death compared to the uncertainties that surround the whole brain dysfunction criterion.

It should be clear by now that the answer to the question "When is someone dead?" is not as straightforward as it might at first seem. Those in the natural law tradition agree that death occurs with the irreversible cessation of integrated organic functioning and, although many think this occurs with the death of the brain, some hold that the only fully reliable criterion for death is the irreversible cessation of respiration and heartbeat.[2]

Other vexed ethical questions surrounding transplantation abound, some of which, such as proposals for "presumed consent" laws and for allowing the buying and selling of organs, we mentioned at the beginning of this chapter. One other question that we should mention, because of its obvious relevance to the definition of death, concerns the controversial practice of "donation after cardiac death." How much time should elapse between the cessation of heartbeat and the removal of the heart or other vital organs for transplantation? Some transplant surgeons wait only a few minutes. Is this sufficient to ensure that the cessation of heartbeat is irreversible (see Kaczor 2011)?

In conclusion, the debate about the determination of death is very much alive. One wonders how many of the thousands of people who have consented to their organs being taken after they are "dead," whether this is determined on the basis of whole brain death or cardiac death, know that issue is so contested and controversial. And if they do not know, can they be said to be making a truly informed and autonomous decision?

Notes

1. There is the further concern that the coordination of these subsystems is now being maintained through external causes, such as a ventilator, and can only be maintained through these external causes. Life requires not only integration but *self*-integration. With the help of machines, organs in a laboratory could be made to function in a coordinated way if connected to each other, but that would not make them a unified whole.

2. For an interesting collection of essays, see Jensen (2011). See also Lee and Grisez (2012).

EPILOGUE

This book has sought to introduce the reader to an important but often and unfairly neglected framework for bioethical reflection. It is a framework indebted to some of the greatest minds in Western philosophy, past and present, that can trace its origins to the ancient Greeks and their eagerness to discover something crucial to leading a truly flourishing life: a correct appreciation and understanding of the fundamental human goods. If we get the goods right, we can aim at participating in them and have a reasonable prospect of leading a flourishing life, both humanly and morally. If we get them wrong, or choose against them or neglect them, then we will live a life that is stunted, both humanly and morally.

In any conception of the human goods, life should play a central role both as an end in itself and as an essential means to enjoying the other basic goods. It is hard to deny that one has to be alive to enjoy other goods, and we have noted that, although life sometimes seems to be bad because of the evils affecting it (illness, poverty, abandonment, hopelessness, etc.), the thought experiment of thinking away those evils confirms that life remains, in itself, good and desirable. It follows that efforts to do away with those evils are rational and laudable, whereas attempts to terminate the lives of human beings are anything but.

It is hoped that this modest, introductory book encourages readers to consult the growing literature reflecting the renewed interest in natural law theory and its relevance to the many vital bioethical questions facing the modern world. There are, needless to say, many other bioethical questions beyond the scope of a short volume like this, from questions of justice in the allocation of health care resources; to questions of discrimination in health care provision on the grounds of age, sex, race, and social status; to questions of human "enhancement".[1] The fact that such issues have not been addressed here does not mean natural law ethics does not bear on them and has nothing to say about them. On the contrary, natural law ethics has much to contribute on these issues, not least by articulating and defending the key notion of the fundamental equality of all human beings, especially the most vulnerable, including the dying, patients with advanced dementia, those in

PVS, the frail elderly, those with severe learning disabilities, the disabled newborn, the unborn, and the embryonic human being in the laboratory freezer or dish. Given that both of the dominant approaches to bioethics in universities and colleges today—utilitarianism and principlism—openly reject that belief in fundamental equality, the need for and importance of the natural law voice in the bioethical conversation has never been greater.

Note

1. Reflecting the philosophical richness of natural law thought, there are also many vital questions beyond the scope of bioethics on which it has long made, and continues to make, an important contribution, such as questions of criminal justice and war, including the possession and use of nuclear weapons, and questions of social justice.

Appendix A

The Status of the Human Embryo

Statement of Professor George (Joined by Dr. Gómez-Lobo),
in *Human Cloning*. 2002. Report of the President's Council on
Bioethics. Washington, DC: Appendix.

The subject matter of the present report is human cloning, the production of a human embryo by means of somatic cell nuclear transfer (SCNT) or similar technologies. Just as fertilization, if successful, generates a human embryo, cloning produces the same result by combining what is normally combined and activated in fertilization, that is, the full genetic code plus the ovular cytoplasm. Fertilization produces a new and complete, though immature, human organism. The same is true of successful cloning. Cloned embryos therefore ought to be treated as having the same moral status as other human embryos.

A human embryo is a whole living member of the species *homo sapiens* in the earliest stage of his or her natural development. Unless denied a suitable environment, an embryonic human being will by directing its own integral organic functioning develop himself or herself to the next more mature developmental stage, i.e., the fetal stage. The embryonic, fetal, infant, child, and adolescent stages are stages in the development of a determinate and enduring entity—a human being—who comes into existence as a single cell organism and develops, if all goes well, into adulthood many years later.[1]

Human embryos possess the epigenetic primordia for self-directed growth into adulthood, with their determinateness and identity fully intact. The adult human being that is now you or me is the same human being who, at an earlier stage of his or her life, was an adolescent, and before that a child, an infant, a fetus, and an embryo. Even in the embryonic stage, you and I were undeniably whole, living members of the species *homo sapiens*. We were then, as we are now, distinct and complete (though in the beginning we were, of course, immature) human organisms; we were not mere parts of other organisms.

Consider the case of ordinary sexual reproduction. Plainly, the gametes whose union brings into existence the embryo are not whole or distinct organisms. They are functionally (and not merely genetically) identifiable as *parts* of the male or female (potential) parents. Each has only half the genetic material needed to guide the development of an immature human being toward full maturity. They are destined either to combine with an oocyte or spermatozoon to generate a new and distinct organism, or simply die. Even when fertilization occurs, they do not survive; rather, their genetic material enters into the composition of a new organism.

But none of this is true of the human embryo, from the zygote and blastula stages onward. The combining of the chromosomes of the spermatozoon and of the oocyte generates what every authority in human embryology identifies as a new and distinct organism. Whether produced by fertilization or by SCNT or some other cloning technique, the human embryo possesses all of the genetic material needed to inform and organize its growth. Unless deprived of a suitable environment or prevented by accident or disease, the embryo is actively developing itself to full maturity. The direction of its growth is *not extrinsically determined*, but is in accord with the genetic information *within* it.[2] The human embryo is, then, a whole (though immature) and distinct human organism—a human being.

If the embryo were not a complete organism, then what could it be? Unlike the spermatozoa and the oocytes, it is not a part of the mother or of the father. Nor is it a disordered growth such as a hydatidiform mole or teratoma. (Such entities lack the internal resources to actively develop themselves to the next more mature stage of the life of a human being.) Perhaps someone will say that the early embryo is an intermediate form, something that regularly emerges into a whole (though immature) human organism but is not one yet. But what could cause the emergence of the whole human organism, and cause it with regularity? It is clear that from the zygote stage forward, the major development of this organism is *controlled and directed from within*, that is, by the organism itself. So, after the embryo comes into being, no event or series of events occur that could be construed as the production of a new organism; that is, nothing extrinsic to the developing organism itself acts on it to produce a new character or new direction in development.

But does this mean that the human embryo is a human being deserving of full moral respect such that it may not legitimately be used as a mere means to benefit others?

To deny that embryonic human beings deserve full respect, one must suppose that not every whole living human being is deserving of full respect. To do that, one must hold that those human beings who deserve full respect deserve it not in virtue of *the kind of entity they are*, but, rather, in virtue of some acquired characteristic that some human beings (or human beings at some stages) have and others do not, and which some human beings have in greater degree than others.[3]

We submit that this position is untenable. It is clear that one need not be *actually* conscious, reasoning, deliberating, making choices, etc., in order to be a human being who deserves full moral respect, for it is clear that people who are asleep or in reversible comas deserve such respect. So, if one denied that human beings are intrinsically valuable in virtue of what they are, but required an additional attribute, the additional attribute would have to be a capacity of some sort, and, obviously a capacity for certain mental functions. Of course, human beings in the embryonic, fetal, and early infant stages lack immediately exercisable capacities for mental functions characteristically carried out (though intermittently) by most (not all—consider cases of severely retarded children and adults and comatose persons) human beings at later stages of maturity. Still, they possess in radical (= root) form these very capacities. Precisely by virtue of *the kind of entity they are*, they are from the beginning actively developing themselves to the stages at which these capacities will (if all goes well) be immediately exercisable. In this critical respect, they are quite unlike cats and dogs—even adult members of those species. As humans, they are members of a natural kind—the human species—whose embryonic, fetal, and infant members, if not prevented by some extrinsic cause, develop in due course and by intrinsic self-direction the immediately exercisable capacity for characteristically human mental functions. Each new human being comes into existence possessing the internal resources to develop immediately exercisable characteristically human mental capacities—and only the adverse effects on them *of other causes* will prevent their full development. In this sense, even human beings in the embryonic, fetal, and infant stages have the *basic natural* capacity for characteristically human mental functions.

We can, therefore, distinguish two senses of the "capacity" (or what is sometimes referred to as the "potentiality") for mental functions: an immediately exercisable one, and a basic natural capacity, which develops over time. On what basis can one require for the recognition of full moral respect the first sort of capacity, which is an attribute that human beings acquire (if at all) only in the course of development (and may lose before dying), and that some will have in greater degree than others, and not the second, which is possessed by human beings as such? We can think of no good reason or nonarbitrary justification.

By contrast, there are good reasons to hold that the second type of capacity is the ground for full moral respect.

First, someone entertaining the view that one deserves full moral respect only if one has immediately exercisable capacities for mental functions should realize that the developing human being does not reach a level of maturity at which he or she performs a type of mental act that other animals do not perform—even animals such as dogs and cats—until at least several months after birth. A six-week-old baby lacks the *immediately exercisable* capacity to perform characteristically human mental functions. So, if full moral respect were due only to those who possess immediately exercisable capacities for characteristically human mental functions, it would follow that six-week-old infants do not deserve full moral respect. If one further takes the position that beings (including human beings) deserving less than full moral respect may legitimately be dismembered for the sake of research to benefit those who are thought to deserve full moral respect, then one is logically committed to the view that, subject to parental approval, the body parts of human infants, as well as those of human embryos and fetuses, should be fair game for scientific experimentation.

Second, the difference between these two types of capacity is merely a difference between stages along a continuum. The proximate, or immediately exercisable, capacity for mental functions is only the development of an underlying potentiality that the human being possesses simply by virtue of the kind of entity it is. The capacities for reasoning, deliberating, and making choices are gradually developed, or brought toward maturation, through gestation, childhood, adolescence, and so on. But the difference between a being that deserves full moral respect and a being that does not (and can therefore legitimately be dismembered as a means of benefiting others) cannot consist only in the fact that, while both have some feature, one has more of it than the other. A mere *quantitative* difference (having more or less of the same feature, such as the development of a basic natural capacity) cannot by itself be a justificatory basis for treating different entities in *radically* different ways. Between the ovum and the approaching thousands of sperm, on the one hand, and the embryonic human being, on the other hand, there *is* a clear difference in kind. But between the embryonic human being and that same human being at any later stage of its maturation, there is only a difference in degree.

Third, being a whole human organism (whether immature or not) is an either/or matter—a thing either is or is not a whole human being. But the acquired qualities that could be proposed as criteria for personhood come in varying and continuous degrees: there is an infinite number of degrees of the relevant developed abilities or dispositions, such as for self-consciousness, intelligence, or rationality. So, if human beings were worthy of full moral respect only because of such qualities, and not in virtue of the kind of being they are, then, since such qualities come in varying degrees, no account could be given of why basic rights are not possessed by human beings in varying degrees. The proposition that all human beings are created equal would be relegated to the status of a superstition. For example, if developed self-consciousness bestowed rights, then, since some people are more self-conscious than others (i.e., have developed that capacity to a greater extent than others), some people would be greater in dignity than others, and the rights of the superiors would trump those of the inferiors where the interests of the superiors could be advanced at the cost of the inferiors. This conclusion would follow no matter which of the acquired qualities generally proposed as qualifying some human beings (or human beings at some stages) for full respect were selected. Clearly, developed self-consciousness, or desires, or so on, are arbitrarily selected degrees of development of capacities that all human beings possess in (at least) radical form from the coming-into-being of the organism until his or her death. So, it cannot be the case that *some* human beings a*nd not others* are intrinsically valuable by virtue of a certain degree of development. Rather, human beings are intrinsically valuable *in virtue of what (i.e., the kind of being) they are*; and *all* human beings—not just some, and certainly not just those who have advanced sufficiently along the developmental path as to be able to exercise their capacities for characteristically human mental functions—are intrinsically valuable.

Since human beings are intrinsically valuable and deserving of full moral respect in virtue of what they are, it follows that they are intrinsically valuable from the point at which they come into being. Even in the embryonic stage of our lives, each of us was a human being and, as such, worthy of concern and protection. Embryonic human beings, whether brought into existence by union of gametes, SCNT, or other cloning technologies, should be accorded the status of inviolability recognized for human beings in other developmental stages.

Three arguments have been repeatedly advanced in the course of our Council's deliberations in an effort to cast doubt on the proposition that human embryos deserve to be accorded such status.

(1) Some have claimed that the phenomenon of monozygotic twinning shows that the embryo in the first several days of its gestation is not a human individual. The suggestion is that as long as twinning can occur, what exists is not yet a unitary human being but only a mass of cells—each cell is totipotent and allegedly independent of the others.

It is true that *if a cell or group of cells is detached from the whole* at an early stage of embryonic development, then what is detached can sometimes become a distinct organism and has the potential to develop to maturity as distinct from the embryo from which it was detached (this is the meaning of "totipotent"). But this does nothing to show that before detachment the cells within the human embryo constituted only an incidental mass. Consider the parallel case of division of a flatworm. Parts of a flatworm have the potential to become a whole flatworm when isolated from the present whole of which they are part. Yet no one would suggest that prior to the division of a flatworm to produce two whole flatworms the original flatworm was not a unitary individual. Likewise, at the early stages of human embryonic development, before specialization by the cells has progressed very far, the cells or groups of cells can become whole organisms if they are divided and have an appropriate environment after the division. But that fact does not in the least indicate that prior to such an extrinsic division the embryo is other than a unitary, self-integrating, actively developing human organism. It certainly does not show that the embryo is a mere clump of cells.

In the first two weeks, the cells of the developing embryonic human being already manifest a degree of specialization or differentiation. From the very beginning, even at the two-cell stage, the cells differ in the cytoplasm received from the original ovum. Also they are differentiated by their position within the embryo. In mammals, even in the unfertilized ovum, there is already an "animal" pole (from which the nervous system and eyes develop)[4] and a "vegetal" pole (from which the future "lower" organs and the gut develop). After the initial cleavage, the cell coming from the "animal" pole is probably the primordium of the nervous system and the other senses, and the cell coming from the "vegetal" pole is probably the primordium of the digestive system. Moreover, the relative position of a cell from the very beginning (i.e., from the first cleavage) has an impact on its functioning. Monozygotic twinning usually occurs at the blastocyst stage, in which there clearly is a differentiation of the inner cell mass and the trophoblast that surrounds it (from which the placenta develops).[5]

The orientation and timing of the cleavages are species specific, and are therefore genetically determined, that is, determined from within. Even at the two-cell stage, the embryo begins synthesizing a glycoprotein called "E-cadherin" or "uvomorulin," which will be instrumental in the compaction process at the eight-cell stage, the process in which the blastomeres (individual cells of the embryo at the blastocyst stage) join tightly together, flattening and developing an inside-outside polarity.[6] And there is still more evidence, but the point is that from the zygote stage forward, the embryo, as well as maintaining homeostasis, is internally integrating various processes to direct them in an overall growth pattern toward maturity.[7]

But the clearest evidence that the embryo in the first two weeks is not a mere mass of cells but is a unitary organism is this: *if the individual cells within the embryo before twinning were each independent of the others, there would be no reason why each would not regularly develop on its own. Instead, these allegedly independent, noncommunicating cells regularly function together to develop into a single, more mature member of the human species.* This fact shows that interaction is taking place between the cells from the very beginning (even within the zona pellucida, before implantation), restraining them from individually developing as whole organisms and directing each of them to function as a relevant part of a single, whole organism continuous with the zygote. Thus, prior to an extrinsic division of the cells of the embryo, these cells together do constitute a single organism. So, the fact of twinning does not show that the embryo is a mere incidental mass of cells. Rather, the evidence clearly indicates that the human embryo, from the zygote stage forward, is a unitary, human organism.

(2) The second argument we wish to address suggests that since people frequently do not grieve, or do not grieve intensely, for the loss of an embryo early in pregnancy, as they do for the loss of a fetus late in pregnancy or of a newborn, we are warranted in concluding that the early embryo is not a human being worthy of full moral respect.

The absence of grieving is sometimes a result of ignorance about the facts of embryogenesis and intrauterine human development. If people are told (as they still are in some places) that there simply is no human being until "quickening"— a view which is preposterous in light of the embryological facts—then they are likely not to grieve (or not to grieve intensely) at an early miscarriage. But people who are better informed, and women in particular, very often *do* grieve even when a miscarriage occurs early in pregnancy.

Granted, some people informed about many of the embryological facts are nevertheless indifferent to early miscarriages; but this is often due to a reductionist view according to which embryonic human beings are misdescribed as mere "clumps of cells," "masses of tissue," etc. The *emotional* attitude one has toward early miscarriages is typically and for the most part *an effect* of what one thinks— rightly or wrongly—about the humanity of the embryo. Hence, it is circular reasoning to use the indifference of people who deny (wrongly, in our view) that human beings in the embryonic stage deserve full moral respect as an argument for not according such respect.

Moreover, the fact that people typically grieve less in the case of a miscarriage than they do in the case of an infant's death is partly explained by the simple facts that they do not actually see the baby, hold her in their arms, talk to her, and so on. The process of emotional bonding is typically completed after the child is born—sometimes, and in some cultures, months after the child is born. However, a child's right not to be killed plainly does not depend on whether her parents or anyone else has formed an emotional bond with her. Every year—perhaps every day—people die for whom others do not grieve. This does not mean that they lacked the status of human beings who were worthy of full moral respect.

It is simply a mistake to conclude from the fact that people do not grieve, or grieve less, at early miscarriage that the embryo has in herself less dignity or worth than older human beings.

(3) We now turn to the third argument. Some people, apparently, are moved to believe that embryonic human beings are not worthy of full moral respect because a high percentage of embryos formed in natural pregnancies fail to implant or spontaneously abort. Again, we submit that the inference is fallacious.

It is worth noting first, as the standard embryology texts point out, that many of these unsuccessful pregnancies are really due to incomplete fertilizations. So, in many cases, what is lost is not actually a human embryo. To be a complete human organism (a human being), the entity must have the epigenetic primordia for a functioning brain and nervous system, though a chromosomal defect might only prevent development to maximum functioning (in which case it would be a human being, though handicapped). If fertilization is not complete, then what is developing is not an organism with the active capacity to develop itself to the mature (even if handicapped) state of a human.

Second, the argument here rests upon a variant of the naturalistic fallacy. It supposes that what happens in "nature," i.e., with predictable frequency without the intervention of human agency, must be morally acceptable when deliberately caused. Since embryonic death in early miscarriages happens with predictable frequency without the intervention of human agency, the argument goes, we are warranted in concluding that the deliberate destruction of human beings in the embryonic stage is morally acceptable.

The unsoundness of such reasoning can easily be brought into focus by considering the fact that historically, and in some places even today, the *infant* mortality rate has been very high. If the reasoning under review here were sound, it would show that human infants in such circumstances could not be full human beings possessing a basic right not to be killed for the benefit of others. But that of course is surely wrong. The argument is a *non sequitur*.

In conclusion, we submit that law and public policy should proceed on the basis of full moral respect for human beings irrespective of age, size, stage of development, or condition of dependency. Justice requires no less. In the context of the debate over cloning, it requires, in our opinion, a ban on the production of embryos, whether by SCNT or other processes, for research that harms them or results in their destruction. Embryonic human beings, no less than human beings at other developmental stages, should be treated as subjects of moral respect and human rights, not as objects that may be damaged or destroyed for the benefit of others. We also hold that cloning-to-produce-children ought to be legally prohibited. In our view, such cloning, even if it could be done without the risk of defects or deformities, treats the child-to-be as a product of manufacture, and is therefore inconsistent with a due respect for the dignity of human beings. Still, it is our considered judgment that cloning-for-biomedical-research, inasmuch as it involves the deliberate destruction of embryos, is morally worse than cloning-to-produce-children. Thus we urge that any ban on cloning-to-produce-children be a prohibition on the practice of cloning itself, and not on the implantation of embryos. Public policy should protect embryonic human beings and certainly not mandate or encourage their destruction. An effective ban on cloning-to-pro-duce-children would be a ban on all cloning.[8]

Although an optimal policy would permanently ban all cloning, we join in this Council's call for a permanent ban on cloning-to-produce-children com-bined with a four-year ban (or "moratorium") on cloning-for-biomedical-re-search for the reasons set forth by Gilbert Meilaender in his personal statement. It is our particular hope that a four-year period will provide time for a careful and thorough public debate about the moral status of the human embryo. This is a debate we welcome.

* * *

Robert P. George
Alfonso Gómez-Lobo

Notes

Materials produced by the President's Council on Bioethics in this archive are government documents and in the public domain. Please note the source as https://bioethicsarchive.georgetown.edu/pcbe/.

1. A human embryo (like a human being in the fetal, infant, child, or ado-lescent stage) is not properly classified as a "prehuman" organism with the mere potential to become a human being. No human embryologist or textbook in hu-man embryology known to us presents, accepts, or remotely contemplates such a view. The testimony of all leading embryology textbooks is that a human embryo is—already and not merely potentially—a human being. His or her potential, assuming a sufficient measure of good health and a suitable environment, is to develop by an internally directed process of growth through the further stages of maturity on the continuum that is his or her life.

2. The timing of the first two cleavages seems to be controlled by the mater-nal RNA within the embryo rather than by its new DNA (see Ronan O'Rahilly and Fabiola Mueller, *Human Embryology and Teratology* (New York: John Wiley & Sons, 1992), 23). Still, these cleavages do not occur if the embryo's nucleus is not present, and so the nuclear genes also control these early changes.

3. A possible alternative, though one finding little support in current discus-sions, would be to argue that what I am, or you are, is not a human organism at all, but rather a nonbodily consciousness or spirit merely inhabiting or somehow "associated with" a body. The problem with this argument is that it is clear that we are bodily entities-organisms, albeit of a particular type, namely, organisms of a rational nature. A living thing that performs bodily actions is an organism, a bodily entity. But it is immediately obvious in the case of the human individual that it is *the same subject* that perceives, walks, and talks (which are bodily ac-tions), and that understands, deliberates, and makes choices—what everyone, including anyone who denies he is an organism, refers to as "I." It must be the same entity that perceives these words on a page, for example, and understands

them. Thus, what each of us refers to as "I" is identically the physical organism that is the subject both of bodily actions, such as perceiving and walking, and of mental activities, such as understanding and choosing. Therefore, you and I are physical organisms, rather than consciousnesses that merely inhabit or are "associated with" physical organisms. And so, plainly, *we* came to be when the physical organism we are came to be; *we* once were embryos, then fetuses, then infants, and so on.

4. Werner A. Muller, *Developmental Biology* (New York: Springer Verlag, 1997), 12 f. Scott Gilbert, *Developmental Biology* 5th edition (Sunderland, Mass.: Sinnauer Associates, 1997); O'Rahilly and Mueller, *Human Embryology and Teratology*, 23–24.

5. O'Rahilly and Fabiola Mueller, *Human Embryology and Teratology*, 30–31.

6. Ibid., 23–24; Keith Moore and T. V. N. Persaud, *Before We Are Born: Essentials of Embryology and Birth Defects* (Philadelphia: W. B. Saunders, 1998), 41; William J. Larson, *Human Embryology* 3rd edition (New York: Churchill Livingstone, 2001), 18–21.

7. Gilbert, *Developmental Biology*, 12 f; 167 f. Also see O'Rahilly and Mueller, *Human Embryology and Teratology* 23–24.

8. A ban on implantation of an existing embryo or class of embryos would be subject to constitutional as well as moral objections. Such a ban would certainly be challenged, and the challenge would likely come from a powerful coalition of "pro-life" and "pro-choice" forces. A prohibition of the production of embryos by cloning would have a far better likelihood of withstanding constitutional challenge than would a ban on implantation.

Appendix B

The Determination of Death

Personal Statement of Dr. Alfonso Gómez-Lobo. 2008.
In *Controversies in the Determination of Death: A White
Paper Published by the President's Council on Bioethics*.
Washington, DC: Appendix.

The purpose of this statement is to present my personal views on three different
issues that arise within the debate addressed in the present report.

Conceptual Issues

Since the publication of the reports by the Harvard Ad Hoc Committee (1968)
and by the President's Commission (1981), it has become commonplace to claim
that "the definition of death" has been revised, and that, accordingly, the definition "has changed" or "has evolved." It is thus suggested that the medical profession now has an understanding of death that is different from the one it had a
few decades ago. Moreover, the "new definition," the one that "defines" death as
"whole brain death," is the one that has been enshrined in the law.

In my view, this use of the philosophical term "definition" is inaccurate and all
too often seriously misleading.

To define a term is to provide, in other words, an account of its meaning.
Thus, if we define "triangle" as "a plane figure with three straight sides" and the
definition is changed to "a plane figure with four straight sides," then the term
"triangle" will no longer single out triangles, but squares. In fact, a change in
definition usually entails a change in reference. Hence, if the definition of "death"
changes, we will not be referring to the same natural phenomenon we had been
trying to identify before the semantic change took place.

If the contemporary dispute about death is to be intelligible, the definition of
"death" must remain stable.

A long tradition in philosophy with many contemporary defenders points out
that there are two kinds of definitions: ordinary language definitions and specialized language definitions. Most people understand "water" to mean, roughly, "a
transparent liquid that flows from the kitchen or bathroom faucet, and is safe to
drink." However, people with some knowledge of chemistry define it as "a liquid
whose basic molecule is composed of two atoms of hydrogen and one of oxygen."

Likewise, it is reasonable to expect that there will be two kinds of definition
for the term "death." First, "death" as ordinarily understood means "the irreversible cessation of life" and applies to all things that have been alive. There is no
separate definition that applies, say, only to humans, to the exclusion of animals
or plants. Nor can life irreversibly cease more than once. Hence, there is only one
death for each organism. Death, furthermore, is a natural, biological event with

social consequences, not a moral, legal, or political decision on the part of those observing it. Death itself should not be confused with the ruling that death has occurred.

The definition of "death" as "the irreversible cessation of life" is a definition by exclusion. It is a derivative account that is parasitic on the more primitive notion of life. A second, specialized language definition of "death" would thus have to specify, in the language of biology, the essential properties of life. Although progress has been made in the understanding of DNA and other driving factors of life, we are far from being able to give an essential definition of "life" analogous to the H_2O definition of "water." We must resort instead to the observable signs of life. These allow us to state whether an organism is alive or dead. If a body is able to process nutrition, eliminate waste, and exhibit proportional growth, homeostasis, etc., and, moreover, it engages in these functions in an integrated manner, we shall correctly deem it to be alive. If it fails to do this, and starts to decompose and disintegrate, we will rightly judge it to be dead.

In judging as we have just described, we have adopted observable criteria for life. "Criteria" is the plural of "criterion," a word whose Greek roots suggest the idea of separation or distinction. A good example of a criterion is a sieve that separates liquids from solids. A criterion is thus chosen, and is sometimes even man-made. We decide what we will use as a criterion, that is, as an instrument for setting apart the living from the dead. An alternative, synonymous expression commonly used to refer to criteria is the word "standards."

Thus, the appeal to the traditional cardiorespiratory criterion or standard is a choice to determine death by verifying the irreversible cessation of heartbeat and breathing. To choose to determine death by total brain failure does not change the definition of death. It is a decision to use a different standard to determine death.

A standard is chosen, but the choice can be wrong. It depends on what the function of the standard is expected to be. If the goal is to separate liquids from sand, a sieve with large holes will be the wrong choice. Likewise, if a criterion to determine death is chosen that leads us to declare dead certain individuals who continue to display the observable signs of life, then that standard will have been wrongly chosen.

The "higher brain death" criterion or standard for death seems to be a wrong choice for several reasons: it turns on an unpersuasive distinction between the death of plants or animals, and the death of a person. Moreover, it requires us to assume that we undergo two deaths: the death of the mind and the death of the body (although for most people they would be simultaneous events). Furthermore, it leaves behind not a cadaver, but an ostensibly living body.

The choice of a specific criterion or standard is insufficient, by itself, to determine whether someone is dead or alive. A trained, experienced eye must observe whether the conditions specified in the formulation of the standard are or are not objectively present in a patient. To satisfy this diagnostic need, tests are designed to operate under each of the different criteria. To place a stethoscope on the chest of a patient in order to verify whether his or her heart has stopped beating is to conduct a test under the cardiorespiratory standard. To perform an EEG is to conduct one of the tests to establish total brain failure.

Tests can be inaccurate and lead to unclear results, that is, to the conclusion that we are uncertain whether someone is dead or alive.[1] The inaccuracy of tests can also lead to false results, such as declaring dead someone who later recovers. The epistemic question of whether we can be certain that someone is dead or alive leads to further refinement of our tests, and may play a crucial role in reaching a moral judgment, but it should not be confused with the physiological question—whether the brain is the organ responsible for the integrated functioning of the organism, so that total brain failure is the same as the irreversible cessation of the life of a given organism.

Physiological Issues

During the discussion of the present report, evidence was offered that seems to show that survival after total brain failure is not only possible, but has been documented in approximately 175 cases. This would entail "that the body's integrative unity derives from mutual interaction among its parts, not from a top-down imposition of one 'critical organ' upon an otherwise mere bag of organs and tissues."[2]

In order to disprove this last finding, one (or both) of the following two conditions would have to be met:

First, that the "brain dead" individuals who continue to live are not really "brain dead." That is, they would all have to be cases of misdiagnosis of total and irreversible brain failure. Given the evidence adduced (especially the results of a brain autopsy of a patient who survived 20 years after the diagnosis of total brain failure due to bacterial meningitis),[3] it seems to me that there are credible reasons to think that the patients were indeed "brain dead."

And second, that the functions exhibited by the patients are not indicative of the integrated functioning of an organism. In other words, one would have to argue that all observed biological processes were only lingering activations of some subsystems of the body: the body as a whole would not be alive because of its lack of holistic properties. This last claim is contradicted by the fact that, for example, proportional growth and, more generally, homeostasis, and perhaps other observable phenomena, cannot be explained as the isolated functioning of a part of the organism. I think it is reasonable to think that these are holistic properties that involve the organism as a whole.

On the basis of the aforementioned findings, I am inclined to hold that the choice of whole brain failure as a standard for death is a questionable choice, whether it is based on the physiological claim that the brain is the integrative organ for the whole organism or on the general biological claim that the spontaneous drive to breathe, which is dependent on the brain, is necessary for life. The existence of conscious, yet apneic, patients allows us to dispose of the latter claim. Since some apneic individuals are alive, it follows that it appears to be false that all individuals who lack the drive to breathe spontaneously are dead.

With regard to the role of the brain, there is a further physiological consideration to be taken into account. During the early embryonic stages of an organism, there is certainly integrated functioning of subsystems, and this happens before the brain is formed. This suggests that the brain is not the organ that is responsible for the integrated functioning of the organism of which it is a part, but rather that it is itself a product of a prior dynamism of the integrated whole.

From the information presented to me, I am provisionally inclined to side with what in the report is called Position One. I am aware of its minority status, and that it could be overthrown if new evidence shows that either alleged "whole brain dead" patients have been misdiagnosed or that the apparent survival of those patients is only a lingering preservation of uncoordinated physiological subsystems.

Ethical Issues

In my view, the ethical cornerstone of vital organ transplantation is the dead-donor rule: no one should be intentionally killed so that his or her organs may benefit someone else. To violate this rule is to go against the goals of medicine and to violate a basic norm of human interaction.

If a certain standard or criterion, no matter how widely accepted, entails the risk of violating the dead-donor rule, then it should be revised in light of the empirical evidence. If it turns out that the current neurological standard allows, in certain cases, the extraction of organs from individuals who are still alive, then the morally right thing to do would be to abandon it and adopt a safer criterion.

Notes

Materials produced by the President's Council on Bioethics in this archive are government documents and in the public domain. Please note the source as https://bioethicsarchive.georgetown.edu/pcbe/.

1. K. G. Karakatsanis, "'Brain Death': Should It Be Reconsidered?" *Spinal Cord* 46, no. 6 (2008): 396–401.

2. D. A. Shewmon, "Chronic 'Brain Death': Meta-Analysis and Conceptual Consequences," *Neurology* 51, no. 6 (1998): 1538–45.

3. S. Repertinger, W. P. Fitzgibbons, M. F. Omojola, and R. A. Brumback, "Long Survival Following Bacterial Meningitis-Associated Brain Destruction," *J Child Neurol* 21, no. 7 (2006): 591–95.

REFERENCES

Beauchamp, T. L., and J. F. Childress. 2013. *Principles of Biomedical Ethics*. 7th ed. Oxford: Oxford University Press.

Beckwith, F. 2007. *Defending Life: A Moral and Legal Case against Abortion Choice*. Cambridge: Cambridge University Press. http://dx.doi.org/10.1017/CBO9780 511804885.

Bouillon-Jensen, C., and D. R. Larson. 2004. "Infanticide." In *Encyclopedia of Bioethics*, vol. 3, 3rd ed. Edited by S. G. Post, 1236–44. New York: Macmillan Reference USA.

Bradley, G.V. 2003. "Retribution: The Central Aim of Punishment." *Harvard Journal of Law & Public Policy* 27, no. 1: 19–31.

Campbell, N. A., and J. B. Reece. 2002. *Campbell Biology*. 6th ed. San Francisco: Benjamin Cummings.

Cavanaugh, T. A. 2006. *Double Effect Reasoning: Doing Good and Avoiding Evil*. Oxford: Oxford University Press.

Damschen, G., A. Gómez-Lobo, and D. Schönecker. 2006. "Sixteen Days? A Reply to B. Smith and B. Brogaard on the Beginning of Human Individuals." *Journal of Medicine and Philosophy* 31, no. 2: 165–75. http://dx.doi.org /10.1080/03605310600588707. Medline:16595346.

Davies, M. 2014. "Woman Who Had No Idea She Was Pregnant Gives Birth at GP Surgery After Going to Appointment for Stomach Ache," *Daily Mail*, October 22. http://www.dailymail.co.uk/health/article-2802876/woman-no-idea -pregnant-gives-birth-gp-surgery-going-appointment-stomach-ache.html.

Day, M. 2009. "Italy Faces Constitutional Crisis over Coma Woman." *Observer*, February 7. http://www.theguardian.com/world/2009/feb/08/englaro-italy -vatican.

DeGrazia, D. 2005. *Human Identity and Bioethics*. Cambridge: Cambridge University Press.

———. 2006. "Moral Status, Human Identity, and Early Embryos: A Critique of the President's Approach." *Journal of Law, Medicine & Ethics* 34, no. 1: 49–57. http://dx.doi.org/10.1111/j.1748-720X.2006.00008.x. Medline:16489984.

Dellapenna, J. W. 2006. *Dispelling the Myths of Abortion History*. Durham, NC: Carolina Academic Press.

Descartes, R. 1637. *Discourse on Method*. Part IV.

Dworkin, R. 1994. *Life's Dominion: An Argument about Abortion, Euthanasia and Individual Freedom*. New York: Vintage Books.

Edwards, R.G., and P. Steptoe. 1981. *A Matter of Life*. London: Sphere Books.

Engelhardt, H. T. 1996. *The Foundations of Bioethics*. 2nd ed. Oxford: Oxford University Press.

Finnis, J. 1983. *Fundamentals of Ethics*. Washington, DC: Georgetown University Press.

————. 1993. "*Bland*: Crossing the Rubicon?" *Law Quarterly Review* 109:329–37. Medline:11652844.

————. 2010. "The Other F-Word." *Public Discourse*, October 20. http://www .thepublicdiscourse.com/2010/10/1849/.

————. 2011a. "Intention and Side Effects." In *Intention and Identity: Collected Essays*, vol. 2, ed. J. Finnis, 173–97. Oxford: Oxford University Press. http://dx .doi.org/10.1093/acprof:oso/9780199580064.003.0011.

————. 2011b. *Natural Law and Natural Rights*. 2nd ed. Oxford: Oxford University Press.

————. 2011c. "On Producing Human Embryos." In *Intention and Identity: Collected Essays*, vol. 2, ed. J. Finnis, 293–301. Oxford: Oxford University Press. http://dx.doi.org/10.1093/acprof:oso/9780199580064.003.0018.

————. 2013. "Capacity, Harm and Experience in the Life of Persons as Equals." *Journal of Medical Ethics* 39, no. 5: 281–3. http://dx.doi.org/10.1136/medeth ics-2012-101198.

————, J. Boyle, and G. Grisez. 1988. *Nuclear Deterrence, Morality and Realism*. Oxford: Oxford University Press.

————, and A. Fisher. 1994. "Theology and Four Principles of Bioethics: A Roman Catholic View." In *Principles of Health Care Ethics*, ed. R. Gillon, 31–44. Chichester, UK: Wiley.

Fisher, A. 2013. "Bioethics after Finnis." In *Reason, Morality and Law. The Philosophy of John Finnis*, ed. J. Keown and R. P. George, 269–89. Oxford: Oxford University Press. http://dx.doi.org/10.1093/acprof:oso/9780199675500.003.0018.

Fisher, A., and L. Gormally. 2001. *Healthcare Allocation: An Ethical Framework for Public Policy*. London: Linacre Centre.

Fitzpatrick, F. J. 1988. *Ethics in Nursing Practice: Basic Principles and Their Application*. London: Linacre Centre.

Frith, M. 2014. "You're Big Business Now, Baby." *Daily Telegraph*, October 19. http://www.telegraph.co.uk/women/womens-health/11171311/Youre-big -business-now-baby.html.

George, R. P. 1995. *Making Men Moral: Civil Liberties and Public Morality*. Oxford: Oxford University Press. http://dx.doi.org/10.1093/acprof:oso/9780198 260240.001.0001.

George, R. P., and C. Tollefsen. 2011. *Embryo: A Defense of Human Life*. 2nd ed. Princeton, NJ: Witherspoon Institute.

Gillon, R. 1986. *Philosophical Medical Ethics*. Chichester, UK: Wiley.

————, ed. 1994. *Principles of Health Care Ethics*. Chichester, UK: Wiley.

Giubilini, A., and F. Minerva. 2013. "After-Birth Abortion: Why Should the Baby Live?" *Journal of Medical Ethics* 39, no. 5: 261–63. http://dx.doi.org/10.1136 /medethics-2011-100411.

Glannon, W. 2005. *Biomedical Ethics*. Oxford: Oxford University Press.

Glover, J. 1991. *Causing Death and Saving Lives*. London: Penguin.

Gómez-Lobo, A. 2002. *Morality and the Human Goods. An Introduction to Natural Law Ethics*. Washington, DC: Georgetown University Press.

———. 2004a. "Does Respect for Embryos Entail Respect for Gametes?" *Theoretical Medicine* 25, no. 3: 199–208. http://dx.doi.org/10.1023/B:META.000004 0038.52317.08. Medline:15529806.

———. 2004b. "On the Ethical Evaluation of Stem Cell Research: Remarks on a Paper by N. Knoepffler." *Kennedy Institute of Ethics Journal* 14, no. 1: 75–80. http://dx.doi.org/10.1353/ken.2004.0015. Medline:15250119.

———. 2005. "On Potentiality and Respect for Embryos: A Reply to Mary Mahowald." *Theoretical Medicine* 26, no. 2: 105–10. http://dx.doi.org/10.1007/s11 017-005-1235 9.

———. 2007. "Individuality and Human Beginnings: A Reply to David DeGrazia." *Journal of Law, Medicine & Ethics* 35, no. 3: 457–62. http://dx.doi.org /10.1111/j.1748-720X.2007.00167.x. Medline:17714254.

———. 2008. "Inviolability at Any Age." *Kennedy Institute of Ethics Journal* 17, no. 4: 311–20. http://dx.doi.org/10.1353/ken.2008.0008.

Gray, K., and S. F. Gray. 2009. *Elements of Land Law*. 5th ed. Oxford: Oxford University Press.

Guenin, L. M. 2008. *The Morality of Embryo Use*. Cambridge: Cambridge University Press.

Hough, A. 2012. "1.7 Million Human Embryos Created For IVF Thrown Away." *Daily Telegraph*, December 31. http://www.telegraph.co.uk/news/health/news /9772233/1.7-million-human-embryos-created-for-IVF-thrown-away.html.

Jackson, E., and J. Keown. 2011. *Debating Euthanasia*. Oxford: Hart Publishing.

Jaenisch, R. 2004. "The Biology of Nuclear Cloning and the Potential of Embryonic Stem Cells for Transplantation Therapy." Appendix N to *Monitoring Stem Cell Research. A Report of the President's Council on Bioethics*, 385–414. Washington DC: President's Council on Bioethics. https://bioethicsarchive.george town.edu/pcbe/reports/stemcell/index.html.

Jensen, S. J. 2011. *The Ethics of Organ Transplantation*. Washington, DC: Catholic University of America Press.

Kaczor, C. 2011. "Organ Donation Following Cardiac Death: Conflicts of Interest, Ante Mortem Interventions, and Determinations of Death." In *The Ethics of Organ Transplantation*, ed. S. J. Jensen, 95–113. Washington, DC: Catholic University of America Press.

———. 2013. *A Defense of Dignity. Creating Life, Destroying Life, and Protecting the Rights of Conscience*. Notre Dame, IN: University of Notre Dame Press.

———. 2015. *The Ethics of Abortion. Women's Rights, Human Life and the Question of Justice*. 2nd ed. New York: Routledge.

Kant, I. 2012. *Kant: Groundwork of the Metaphysics of Morals*. 2nd ed. Edited by M. Gregor and J. Timmermann. Cambridge: Cambridge University Press.

Kennedy, I., and A. Grubb. 1994. *Medical Law: Text with Materials*. 2nd ed. London: Butterworths.

Keown, D. 2001. *Buddhism and Bioethics*. Basingstoke, UK: Palgrave Macmillan.

Keown, J. 1988. *Abortion, Doctors and the Law*. Cambridge: Cambridge University Press. http://dx.doi.org/10.1017/CBO9780511563683.

———. 1995. "Review of Kennedy, I., and Grubb, A. *Medical Law: Text with Materials.*" *Cambridge Law Journal* 54:190–92. http://dx.doi.org/10.1017/S00081 97300083306.

———. 1997. "Restoring Moral and Intellectual Shape to the Law after *Bland.*" *Law Quarterly Review* 113:481–503. Medline:12962086.

———. 2002. *Euthanasia, Ethics and Public Policy.* Cambridge: Cambridge University Press.

———. 2012. *The Law and Ethics of Medicine. Essays on the Inviolability of Human Life.* Oxford: Oxford University Press. http://dx.doi.org/10.1093/acprof :oso/9780199589555.001.0001.

———, and R. P. George, eds. 2013. *Reason, Morality and Law: The Philosophy of John Finnis.* Oxford: Oxford University Press. http://dx.doi.org/10.1093/acpro f:oso/9780199675500.001.0001.

King, M. L. 1963. "Letter from a Birmingham Jail." Martin Luther King, Jr. Research and Education Institute, https://kinginstitute.stanford.edu/king-papers /documents/letter-birmingham-jail.

Knapton, S. 2015. "New Era of Medicine Begins as First Children Cured of Genetic Disorder." *Daily Telegraph,* April 21.

Lee, P. 2010. *Abortion and Unborn Human Life.* 2nd ed. Washington, DC: Catholic University of America Press.

Lee, P., and R. P. George. 2008. *Body-Self Dualism in Contemporary Ethics and Politics.* Cambridge: Cambridge University Press.

Lee, P., and G. Grisez. 2012. "Total Brain Death: A Reply to Alan Shewmon." *Bioethics* 26, no. 5: 275–84. http://dx.doi.org/10.1111/j.1467-8519.2010.01846.x . Medline:22724128.

Mahowald, M. B. 2004. "Respect for Embryos and the Potentiality Argument." *Theoretical Medicine* 25, no. 3: 209–14. http://dx.doi.org/10.1023/B:META .0000040065.84498.4c.

Marquis, D. 1989. "Why Abortion Is Immoral." *Journal of Philosophy* 86, no. 4: 183–202. http://dx.doi.org/10.2307/2026961. Medline:11782094.

McMahan, J. 1999. "Cloning, Killing, and Identity." *Journal of Medical Ethics* 25, no. 2: 77–86. http://dx.doi.org/10.1136/jme.25.2.77. Medline:10226909.

———. 2002. *The Ethics of Killing: Problems at the Margins of Life.* Oxford: Oxford University Press. http://dx.doi.org/10.1093/0195079981.001.0001.

Moore, K. L., T. V. N. Persaud, and M. G. Torchia. 2011. *The Developing Human: Clinically Oriented Embryology,* 9th ed. Philadelphia: Elsevier Saunders.

Napier, S., ed. 2011. *Persons, Moral Worth and Embryos: A Critical Analysis of Pro-Choice Arguments.* New York: Springer.

Novak, D. 2007. *The Sanctity of Human Life.* Washington, DC: Georgetown University Press.

Oderberg, D. S. 2000a. *Applied Ethics: A Non-Consequentialist Approach.* Oxford: Wiley-Blackwell.

———. 2000b. *Moral Theory: A Non-Consequentialist Approach.* Oxford: Wiley-Blackwell.

Oderberg, D.S., and J.A. Laing, eds. 1997. *Human Lives: Critical Essays on Conse-quentialist Ethics*. New York: St. Martin's Press.

Pearson, H. 2002. "Your Destiny, from Day One." *Nature* 418 (6893): 14–15. http://dx.doi.org/10.1038/418014a. Medline:12097880.

Pellegrino, E. D., and D. C. Thomasma. 1988. *For the Patient's Good: The Restoration of Beneficence in Health Care*. Oxford: Oxford University Press.

———. 1993. *The Virtues in Medical Practice*. Oxford: Oxford University Press.

Prentice, D., and R. Macrito. 2013. *Stem Cells, Cloning and Human Embryos: Understanding the Ethics and Opportunity of Scientific Research*. Washington, DC: Family Research Council; http://downloads.frc.org/EF/EF13E47.pdf.

President's Council on Bioethics. 2002. *Human Cloning and Human Dignity*. Washington, DC: https://bioethicsarchive.georgetown.edu/pcbe/topics/cloning_index.html.

———. 2008. *Human Dignity and Bioethics: Essays Commissioned by the President's Council on Bioethics*. Washington, DC: President's Council on Bioethics. https://bioethicsarchive.georgetown.edu/pcbe/reports/human_dignity/index.html.

Princeton. 2010. "Open Hearts, Open Minds and Fair-Minded Words. A Conference on Life and Choice in the Abortion Debate. 15 and 16 October 2010." Panel two: Debate between John Finnis, Margaret Little, and Peter Singer on the Moral Status of the Fetus. https://webspace.princeton.edu/xythoswfs/webview/fileManager?stk=5A1C39D2CDBE233&entryName=%2Fusers%2Fvalues%2FOther+Searches%2FOpenHeartsOpenMinds&msgStatus= (the file of 374.4 MB).

Sadler, T.W. 1990. *Langman's Medical Embryology*. 6th ed. Baltimore: Williams & Wilkins.

Shewmon, D.A. 1998. "Chronic 'Brain Death': Meta-Analysis and Conceptual Consequences." *Neurology* 51, no. 6: 1538–45. http://dx.doi.org/10.1212/WNL.51.6.1538.

———. 2001. "The Brain and Somatic Integration: Insights into the Standard Biological Rationale for Equating 'Brain Death' with Death." *Journal of Medicine and Philosophy* 26, no. 5: 457–78. http://dx.doi.org/10.1076/jmep.26.5.457.3000.

———. 2011. "Controversies Surrounding Brain Death." In *The Ethics of Organ Transplantation*, ed. S.J. Jensen, 21–42. Washington, DC: Catholic University of America Press.

Singer, P. 1996. *Rethinking Life and Death: The Collapse of Our Traditional Ethics*. New York: St. Martin's Griffin.

———. 2011. *Practical Ethics*. 3rd ed. Cambridge: Cambridge University Press.

Smart, J. J. C., and B. Williams. 1973. *Utilitarianism: For and Against*. Cambridge: Cambridge University Press.

Smith, B., and B. Brogaard. 2003. "Sixteen Days." *Journal of Medicine and Philosophy* 28, no. 1: 45–78. http://dx.doi.org/10.1076/jmep.28.1.45.14172. Medline:12715281.

Snead, O. C. 2005. "The (Surprising) Truth about Schiavo: A Defeat for the Cause of Autonomy." In *Scholarly Works.* Paper 88. http://scholarship.law.nd.edu /cgi/viewcontent.cgi?article=1093&context=law_faculty_scholarship.

Spitzer, R. J. 2011. *Ten Universal Principles. A Brief Philosophy of the Life Issues.* San Francisco: Ignatius Press.

Thomson, J. J. 1971. "A Defense of Abortion." *Philosophy & Public Affairs* 1, no. 1: 47–66.

Tollefsen, C. O. 2008. *Biomedical Research and Beyond: Expanding the Ethics of Inquiry.* New York: Routledge.

Tooley, M. 1983. *Abortion and Infanticide.* Oxford: Oxford University Press.

UK Department of Health. 2009. *The Pregnancy Book.* http://www.cuh.org.uk /rosie-links-leaflets/department-health-pregnancy-book.

United Nations. 1959. "Declaration of the Rights of the Child". http://www.uni cef.org/malaysia/1959-Declaration-of-the-Rights-of-the-Child.pdf.

Veatch, R. M. 2005. "The Death of Whole-Brain Death: The Plague of the Disaggregators, Somaticists, and Mentalists." *Journal of Medicine and Philosophy* 30, no. 4: 353–78. http://dx.doi.org/10.1080/03605310591008504. Medline:16 029987.

———. 2012. *The Basics of Bioethics.* 3rd ed. Upper Saddle River, NJ: Pearson.

Warren, M. A. 1973. "On the Moral and Legal Status of Abortion." *The Monist* 57, no. 4: 1–9.

Watt, H. 2000. *Life and Death in Healthcare Ethics: A Short Introduction.* London: Routledge.

World Health Organization. 2014. "Female Genital Mutilation." Fact sheet no. 241, February. http://www.who.int/mediacentre/factsheets/fs241/en/.

INDEX

abortion, xiii–n7, 22–23, 37, 50–63, 65n6, 66n17. *See also* preimplantation genetic diagnosis (PGD)
accident, 29, 32
action theory, 4
act utilitarianism, 18. *See also* utilitarianism
adoption, 57–58
adulthood, 29, 41
advance directive, 84, 85
allocation, of health care resources, xxiv–n1
amputation, 12, 80
antibiotics, in persistent vegetative state, 87
Aquinas, xiii–n5, 11
Aristotle, 34n2, 36
autonomous suicide, 67, 70–71
autonomy, 21–25; abortion and, 56–57; euthanasia and, 75–76; physician-assisted suicide and, 73; preimplantation genetic diagnosis and, 46–48; tube feeding and, 85
awareness: in dualist view, 31; harm and, 12, 48; of unborn child, 53. *See also* consciousness

Beauchamp, Tom, xx
beginning-of-life: abortion and, 50–59; preimplantation genetic diagnosis and, 46–50; principle of double effect and, 61–63
being, in ontology, 27
beneficence: in consequentialism, 15; euthanasia and, 75–76; justice and, 19; in nonconsequentialism, 19; preimplantation genetic diagnosis and, 47; as principle, 8–9, 10; in stem cell example, 13, 25
bioethics: beyond doctor-patient relationship, xxiii–n1; defined, xvii;

ethics in, xix–xx; medical ethics vs., xix; natural law in, xxi–xxii; ontology in, xix–xx
blameworthiness, 4–5
Bland, Tony, 81, 88n5
body: in death, 83; integration of, 96; in ontology, 33–34; organ transplantation and, 94–95; in persistent vegetative state, 83
"bottom-up" morality, 5–6
brain, 33–34
"brain dead," 82, 92, 93–96

casuistry, 5–6
change, 29, 32, 36, 52
Childress, James, xx
China, 64
civil law, natural law vs., 8
cloning, xviii, 36, 40
comatose patient, rape of, 17. *See also* persistent vegetative state (PVS)
common morality, 8–9, 9n3, 10
community, 7–8, 20
conscience, principle of, 23, 73–74
consciousness: abortion and, 55, 58; death and, 94–96; harm and, 12; personhood and, 28, 34
consent, 17, 21–22, 80, 89–90, 97
consequentialism, 15–19, 25–26, 26n2, 42, 49, 50
considered opinions, 5, 6
criteria, for death, 93–95

"dead donor rule," 89–91
death: in abortion, 55, 56, 59, 61–63; determination of, 91–97; in euthanasia, 74–75, 77; as harm, 13, 16; organ transplantation and, 89–90; in physician-assisted suicide, 71–72; in suicide, 70–71; tube feeding and, 85

122   *Index*